THE HOME-MADE
SWEET SHOP

THE HOME-MADE
SWEET SHOP

Make your own irresistible confectionery with 90 classic recipes for sweets, candies and chocolates, shown in more than 450 stunning photographs

Claire Ptak

photography by Nicki Dowey

aqua marine

For Damian Blue Thomas

This edition is published by Aquamarine,
an imprint of Anness Publishing Ltd, Blaby Road, Wigston,
Leicestershire LE18 4SE; info@anness.com

www.aquamarinebooks.com; www.annesspublishing.com

If you like the images in this book and would like to investigate
using them for publishing, promotions or advertising, please
visit our website www.practicalpictures.com
for more information.

Publisher: Joanna Lorenz
Senior Editor: Lucy Doncaster
Editor: Kate Eddison
Copy Editor: Catherine Best
Photographer: Nicki Dowey
Food Stylist: Claire Ptak
Food Stylist's Assistants: Kate McCullough
  and Adriana Nascimento
Prop Stylists: Wei Tang and Marianne de Vries
Designer: Lisa Tai
Proofreading Manager: Lindsay Zamponi
Production Controller: Pirong Wang

© Anness Publishing Ltd 2012

A CIP catalogue record for this book is available from
the British Library.

NOTES

Bracketed terms are intended for American readers.
For all recipes, quantities are given in both metric and imperial
measures and, where appropriate, in standard cups and
spoons. Follow one set of measures, but not a mixture,
because they are not interchangeable.

Standard spoon and cup measures are level.
1 tsp = 5ml, 1 tbsp = 15ml, 1 cup = 250ml/8fl oz.
Australian standard tablespoons are 20ml.
Australian readers should use 3 tsp in place of 1 tbsp for
measuring small quantities.
American pints are 16fl oz/2 cups. American readers should
use 20fl oz/2.5 cups in place of 1 pint when measuring liquids.

Electric oven temperatures in this book are for conventional
ovens. When using a fan oven, the temperature will probably
need to be reduced by about 10–20°C/20–40°F. Since ovens
vary, you should check with your manufacturer's instruction
book for guidance.

The nutritional analysis (see page 156) given for each recipe is
calculated per amount (i.e. total weight), unless otherwise
stated. If the recipe gives a range, such as Serves 4–6, then
the nutritional analysis will be for the smaller portion size,
i.e. 6 servings. The analysis does not include optional
ingredients, such as salt added to taste.

Medium (US large) eggs are used unless otherwise stated.

PUBLISHER'S NOTE

CONTENTS

♥

The history of sugar and sweets

In every corner of the world, people delight in buying, making and sharing sweet treats – both for special occasions and as more regular indulgences. Offered as small tokens of appreciation to old friends or used as an introduction to new ones, sweets and candies can put smiles on tearful faces, reward good behaviour in children and soothe broken hearts. Although many sweets are made with sugar, some make use of honey, the first sweetener, or other non-refined sources, all of which lend their own unique flavour and character to the individual confections.

Sugar is the central ingredient in most types of sweet- and candy-making, and it is available in a multitude of forms: from honey to malted grains, from fruit juices to dried fruits, and from cane sugar to syrup tapped from trees.

Honey: the first sweetener

Sweeteners have been used throughout human history to enhance the flavour of foods and, in some cases, for medicinal purposes. The first of these was honey, a natural sugar that is the product of bees. The practice of honey-harvesting dates back many thousands of years, as is demonstrated by a cave painting in Spain that dates from at least 10,000 years ago, which shows a determined man collecting honeycombs from a hole in a cliff wall as wild bees circle round his head.

One of honey's first uses was probably in mead, a fermented drink made from honey and water, which has been said to inspire poets, politicians and priests, among others. This drink was offered to the gods in ancient Egypt, and they believed that bees were formed from the teardrops of Ra, the Sun God, and honey was his gift to mankind. Used as currency to pay taxes, honey clearly had commercial value, and pots of the precious golden liquid were found buried with the pharaohs and hives were found in the Sun Temple. Bees made an appearance in hieroglyphs during the 3rd and 4th centuries BC, which is around the time people first began to keep them and, by 2500BC, Egyptians are known to have been making moulded confections using honey.

The ancient cultures of Babylon, Assyria, Persia, India, Greece and Rome all kept bees, but not every landscape provided the floral banquet the bees needed to thrive. In order to overcome this, hives were moved by camel, mule or cart to better locations.

An alternative mode of transport was also used by the Greeks, Romans, and even 19th-century English beekeepers, who created floating beehives. Loading the hives on to rafts or schooners, they drifted with them upstream or down river to allow the bees to take advantage of more verdant lands during the day, then return to the hives at night.

Other evidence of the uses of honey include earthenware colanders from the Neolithic period, which were discovered in Switzerland. Similar to utensils used today in the Alps to strain honey, they forge a link between past and present.

Today honey remains popular around the world, although with bees under threat it is becoming increasingly precious. Bee-keeping has seen a resurgence in recent years, and honey is frequently used as a natural remedy for all kinds of ailments, from sore throats and tickly coughs to burns and cuts. It is widely used in cooking, adding sweetness and flavour to all manner of sweet and savoury dishes.

Left This 15th-century Illustration from Grand Herbier shows that bees were kept in medieval times.

Below Honey was the original sweetener and is still used in many recipes today.

Above Sugar cane was cultivated and processed in the Caribbean. (The Crusher Squeezes Juice from the Cane, *Antigua, 1823, by William Clark.*)

Other unrefined sugar sources include maple syrup and maple sugar, palm sugar, birch syrup, gur, panela date sugar, agave nectar, fresh fruit and berries, and malted grains. These are most commonly used in the countries where the raw ingredients grow, but with the globalization of cuisines they are becoming increasingly available.

Sugar: sweetest of all

Despite honey's widespread appeal and value, it was sugar that would become one of the world's most prized ingredients. Originating in Polynesia around 5000 years ago, sugar cane was transported to the coastal regions of India, but remained a well-kept secret for thousands of years. In 510BC, however, Emperor Darius of Persia invaded India and discovered that the people there were harvesting an even sweeter crop than honey, one he would call 'the reed which gives honey without bees'. Local people had developed a method for extracting the sweet sap from the cane and used it in food preparation, including the making of confections similar to nougat and marzipan.

The Emperor returned to Persia bearing his sweet spoils, and sugar replaced honey there as the sweetener of choice.

The spread of sugar continued in the 4th century AD, when Alexander the Great encountered the canes in western Asia. Trading routes were established and sugar was imported as both a luxury and a medicinal commodity. The Arab invasion of Persia in the 8th century AD further increased the reach of the sweetener, as the Arabs established sugar cane production along the route of their conquests, which included North Africa, Sicily, Spain and the south of France.

Despite its appearance in so many regions of the world, sugar production remained limited, and during the Middle Ages it was very expensive. Determined to increase the production of such a prized crop, the Spanish and Portuguese in particular determined to find new places in which to cultivate it. With such a goal in mind, Christopher Columbus brought sugar cane cuttings with him to San Domingo in 1493, on his second voyage to the New World. With ideal growing conditions, this tropical island in the Caribbean Sea proved to be the perfect place in which to grow the crop.

Due to reports of this success, the West Indies were rapidly colonized, becoming the centre of sugar production in the world. British, French and Dutch farmers started growing the canes in Brazil, Cuba, Mexico and the West Indies, relying initially on local labour, but later, and regrettably, on slaves from Africa. By the late 18th century, the cane sugar industry was so lucrative that the product was dubbed 'white gold'.

Cane sugar held sway in Europe until the Napoleonic wars in 1793–1815. During this period, blockades prevented imports from the plantations, and farmers turned to sugar beet, an indigenous crop from which German scientist Andreas Marggraf had succeeded in extracting sugar in 1747. Being suited to the European climate (coupled with the abolition of slavery on the plantations), sugar from beet became dominant. The difficulties of importing cane sugar during World War I enhanced the viability of sugar from home-grown beet, and its production and refinement became major industries. Today about 30 per cent of the world's sugar supply comes from beets.

Above Fresh sugar cane.

From cane or beet to sugar

The refining of sugar cane is a complicated, multi-step process. The tough, fibrous canes are first crushed to extract the raw syrup, which is then boiled. After the syrup crystallizes, it goes through a centrifugal machine where it separates into dark brown raw sugar and molasses. The raw sugar is then either further refined to produce white granulated, caster (superfine) or icing (confectioners') sugar, or flavoured with added molasses and sold as light muscovado (brown), soft brown or demerara (raw) sugar. All of these have different textures and flavours, and are used to make a range of foods. Some white sugars are sold as 'golden', which means that they have not been bleached. Sugar beets are refined in a similar way, although they only produce white sugar.

Confections made with sugar

The earliest confections were probably honey-coated nuts, seeds or berries. A halvah-like snack made with sesame seeds was eaten as long ago as 3000BC, and versions of it using nuts, semolina and dried fruits were made by the ancient cultures of China, the Middle East and the Mediterranean. Eventually sugar replaced

Above The refining process is used to make various types of sugar, including demerara.

Left Visiting a confectioner's shop was once a luxury reserved for the wealthy, as depicted in this image from 1827.

Below Sweets have always been popular for festive occasions, especially Christmas, as shown on this 19th-century postcard from Germany.

the honey, and egg whites were added to the concoction, resulting in nougats, which in most cases were available only to the wealthy and served only for special occasions. Today, nearly every region of the world has its own version of nougat. In Iran, gaz nougaz contains pistachios and is flavoured with rosewater. A Chinese version contains peanuts and may come wrapped in edible rice paper. It is called torrone in Italy and turron in Spain – both are made with almonds. The Australian version contains macadamias.

By the first century AD, 'sweets' also may have been used as digestives at the end of a large meal or banquet, and by AD700, the practice of disguising the taste of medicines with a sweet flavouring or coating was common. This tradition continues to this day, with tablets being coated in a sugary shell.

Marzipan, a mouldable sugar-and-almond paste confection first made in Egypt, came to prominence in Europe in the 13th century. An ornamental 'sotelty'

(subtlety) scene sculpted from the coloured paste was served at medieval feasts to honour the accomplishments of the host or commemorate a special occasion. Now frequently hand-crafted into fruit and vegetable shapes, marzipan fulfils a decorative function as well being a tasty treat in contemporary celebrations.

By the Renaissance, sugar had become more accessible and the art of sweet-making had risen to an art form, including exquisite centrepieces in the design of churches and castles, sometimes gilded with real gold leaf. Candied fruit peel and even whole candied fruit delighted both courtiers and the common man. Fresh citrus peel cooked in sugar syrup then smothered in sugar remains a popular treat today. The French glaze their freshest fruits in a process that can take a week, and they are known as les fruits nobles.

Another type of sweet found in many cultures is the jelly made from fruit juices or purées, flavoured with fruit and flower essences. Turkish delight was first made in Turkey in the 15th century and was popularized in Britain in the 19th century. An Eastern European version made with quince is called kotonjata. In Spain, the quince paste membrillo is commonly served with cheese.

From penny sweets to prestigious confectioneries

Sweet shops have a special place in the hearts and minds of people the world over, and the words 'penny sweet' or 'penny candy' (though it's no longer quite so inexpensive) still bring a delightful picture to mind. From old-fashioned stores selling salt-water taffy, candy floss (cotton candy) or rock in seaside villages to modern urban outlets, such as Dylan's Candy Bar in New York City, which claims to offer 5,000 kinds of candy, the sight and smell of all that moulded and flavoured sugar can tempt even the most disciplined dieter.

When you're young and enter into a sweet shop glimmering with lollipops, jelly babies, humbugs, toffees and all manner of shaped gum sweets, the possibilities seem limitless. The experience can be as exciting for adults as it is for children. Succumbing to nostalgia, you may choose a timeless classic such as a sherbet fountain or a quarter of pear drops, or you may decide to please your adult palate with some luscious nougat or beautifully presented candied fruit.

Sweets remain as popular today as they always have been, and in addition to the countless varieties from the big manufacturers there are now many retro sweet stores, both on-line and in cities and towns. At home, sweet-making is seeing a come-back, with people wanting to relearn the skills that their ancestors practised. Fudge and toffee are particularly popular and there are innumerable recipes for these treats, but it is just as easy to

Above Traditional sweet shops are still just as thrilling for children and adults as they have always been.

make hard-boiled sweets, marzipan confections, liquorice, meringues and much more.

Sweets and the arts

From the words of Milton and Shakespeare to Roald Dahl's classic children's fiction, sugary treats have made an appearance in literature, film, music, song and dance for many centuries. George Herbert (1593–1633) provides one of the earlier written references to sugar cane: 'Lovely enchanting language, sugar-cane, Honey of roses, whither wilt thou fly?'. On the stage, one of the most famous manifestations of confectionery is *The Nutcracker* ballet, which describes young Clara's dream visit to the Kingdom of Sweets. She and her prince (transformed into a man from a toy nutcracker) encounter the Sugar Plum Fairy, who wears a crown of sugar and a skirt of candy floss. Her retinue includes dancers delectably costumed as candy

Above Charlie and the Chocolate Factory *is set in a lavish world of chocolate and sweets.*

canes, bonbons, taffy clowns, marzipan shepherds and shepherdesses, ribbon candy and chocolate. For any child, the experience is irresistible.

In more recent times, both the book and films of *Charlie and the Chocolate Factory* elevated author Roald Dahl's story to iconic stature, with its depiction of gum-chewing bad girls and cocky little cowboys.

Set in a whimsical confectionery cosmos where a chocolate river flows and everything is edible, the tale of Charlie Bucket and the golden ticket is both a tempting and a cautionary one for sweet- and chocolate-lovers. The Oompa Loompas' songs encourage moderation ('If you're not greedy, you will go far'), but everything else about Willy Wonka's world is lusciously extravagant.

Sweets and sweet shops play a similarly memorable role in the recent *Harry Potter* books and films, with 'Honeydukes' selling a spectacular range of magical treats, including 'Fizzing Whizbees', which make the consumer float, and 'Bertie Bott's Every Flavour Beans', whose flavours range from apple and raspberry to salt, sand and sardine.

These are just a few examples of how sweets and chocolates have captured the imagination of children and adults alike.

The history of chocolate

First used in ancient sacred rituals, chocolate has undergone several transitions over the centuries and remains an important part of many celebrations today. Believed by Mesoamericans to be a gift from the gods, chocolate has always been held in high regard, being used as a currency, an elixir, a nutritional aide and in love potions, and there is little doubt about its ability to lift the spirits and comfort at times of need. With an ever-increasing demand for high-quality, ethically produced bars, it remains one of the world's favourite confections both in and out of the kitchen.

There are many different types of chocolate available on the market today, from bitter couverture and bars with a high cocoa percentage to creamier, mellower versions, and these have various qualities and melting properties that govern how each particular type should be used.

The origin of chocolate in Mesoamerica

The earliest evidence of the existence of the cacao seed, the primary ingredient in chocolate, has been traced back thousands of years in the Amazon region, and it was part of the diet of successive Mesoamerican civilizations, including the Olmec, Mayan, Toltec and Aztec peoples who lived in what is now the area between central Mexico and Nicaragua. The low-growing cacao trees flourished as wild plants in the rainforest, but may have been cultivated as early as 600BC. Myth has it that the seeds of *quachahuatl*, which produce the cacao tree, were a gift to the Toltec people from Quetzalcoatl, the feathered serpent creator god also known as the 'good god of the garden'.

The sweet pulp may have been the first part of the plant to be eaten, then when wild yeasts in the air converted the sugars in the pulp to alcohol, this fermented version of cacao was drunk with water as a kind of chocolate beer. The pods themselves served as cups.

The seeds, too, changed in the fermenting process, developing a deep, dark, bitter flavour. When they were roasted, they gave off an appealing scent

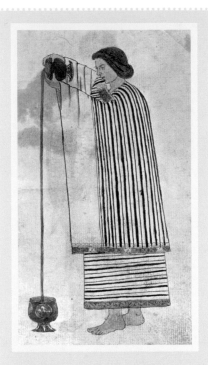

Above This 16th-century vellum artwork from the Codex Tuleda *shows a Mexican Indian preparing chocolate in 1553.*

and provided inspiration once again. Ground in a mortar (*metate*), the roasted seeds were then mixed with vanilla, pepper and spices to make *xocotlatl* or 'bitter water', the cold and frothy forerunner of the modern drink we know as hot chocolate.

Whatever its genesis, the cacao plant was an important talisman. It signified power and rank, and was available to only the loftiest members of the tribes. It was used in religious ceremonies as a divine offering. Drawings on pottery from the period show chocolate being drunk by kings and gods. It was said to have

medicinal and aphrodisiacal benefits, and the Aztecs levied a cacao tax on conquered people and used the humble bean as currency.

Europeans discover chocolate

Cacao beans also exchanged hands along the extensive Mesoamerican trade routes. However, the pleasures and benefits of the plant were unknown in Europe until Christopher Columbus brought some of the New World beans to the Spanish Court in 1502 as souvenirs of his expedition to the territory near Honduras.

The beans paled in comparison to the other treasures he had plundered, and were for the most part ignored. This changed in 1512, when the Aztec king Montezuma II offered a chocolate drink to the Spanish conquistador Hernán Cortés, whom Montezuma believed to be the reincarnation of Quetzalcoatl. Cortés' subsequent treatment of the native Americans was anything but godly, however, as he conquered them and claimed their treasured cacao beans for himself and for Spain. Intrigued by the bracing effect the cacao drink had on his soldiers, Cortés commented that it was a "divine drink which builds up resistance and fights fatigue. A cup of this precious drink permits a man to walk for a whole day without food".

Having returned to Spain with corn, chilli peppers, vanilla, tomatoes, potatoes and a store of cacao seeds, however, Cortés discovered that the Spanish court found the fortifying chocolate drink too astringent. The addition of sugar and vanilla to the ground roasted beans soon resolved this problem and it became very popular, although its consumption was limited to royalty because of its scarcity and the complicated process required to process it. In fact, the Spanish nobility kept the bounty to themselves for some 100 years, until a 17th-century Italian trader brought cacao beans home from his travels to Spain and the West Indies. A chocolate drink called bavaresia was created, and the tradition of Italian chocolate-making was born with its centre in Turin.

From Italy, chocolate fever spread to England, France, Germany, Austria, Switzerland and the Netherlands. A new European passion for the intense hot drink – one that intensified the already strong craving for sugar – was introduced, and the first cocoa-growing colonies were established in Ceylon (British), the West Indies (French), and Venezuela, Java and Sumatra (Dutch).

Above Cocoa plantations, such as this one depicted on the Isle of Grenada, became hugely profitable businesses from the 16th century onwards.

Above Drinking chocolate spread across Europe in the 17th century, including to Switzerland, where The Chocolate Girl *was painted in 1744–5.*

The chocolate revolution

Until the Industrial Revolution began in 1765, chocolate was produced by hand and enjoyed only as a beverage. The introduction of new machinery and improved techniques, however, made mass production of chocolate possible in Britain and then across the rest of Europe. This lowered costs and meant that the general public could finally afford a delicacy that previously had been reserved for only the very wealthy.

Many of the names of the men who transformed the chocolate industry and started prominent businesses are still familiar today. Among them was Conrad Von Houten, a Dutch chemist, who created the first cocoa press in 1815 and who patented a process and a machine that improved the way cocoa butter was separated from chocolate liquor. Not stopping there, he added alkali to the resulting cocoa so that it would mix more easily, creating a method called 'Dutching', which produces darker, milder-flavoured cocoa, and cocoa butter as a by-product.

This discovery was to prove vital to the genesis of the solid chocolate bar, and in 1847 Joseph Fry, an English Quaker, discovered a way to blend cocoa butter with sugar into a paste and form it into a bar that could be eaten without being cooked or mixed with water. This astounding invention led to great success for his company, and Fry's chocolate was one of the major manufacturers of the confection until it morged with Cadbury in the early 20th century.

Meanwhile in Birmingham, John Cadbury, another Quaker and grocer, also started to experiment with roasting and grinding beans to produce chocolate. In 1868, the company became the first to sell boxed chocolates, which were presented in packages decorated with sentimental Victorian illustrations. The company grew and prospered, and in 1879 moved to the Birmingham suburb of Bournville, where it built a factory and a model village for its workers. "The idea," according to Cadbury's great-great-granddaughter Felicity Loudon, was "nobody should ever work or live where a rose cannot grow". Today, Cadbury (now owned by the American company Kraft) is the world's biggest confectionery company.

The other major British player of the time was Rowntree, yet another family of Quaker grocers, whose products competed with those of Fry's and Cadbury's until they were bought out by Nestlé in 1988.

Despite the existence of three such major British producers, it was Switzerland that dominated the chocolate industry throughout the 19th century. The Swiss reputation as premier chocolatiers owes a debt to a trio of its inventive citizens. These were Henri Nestlé, who discovered a way to evaporate milk in 1867; Daniel Peter, with whom Nestlé worked to combine the sweetened condensed milk with chocolate and make the first bar of milk chocolate; and Rudolf Lindt, who in 1879 invented the conching machine, which grinds and smoothes the chocolate liquor, sugar and milk.

In the United States, Milton Hershey was a caramel manufacturer who had already had two failed candy businesses. On an 1893 visit to the World's Columbian Exhibition in Chicago, he was so impressed with German chocolate-making machinery on display that he decided then and there to change course once again.

Above Cacao pods contain seeds and pulp which are fermented before being dried, roasted, winnowed and separated into cocoa solids and cocoa butter.

"Caramels are only a fad," he is reported to have said. "Chocolate is a permanent thing." He located his Pennsylvania factory close to the dairies that would supply milk for his milk chocolate confection. Like John Cadbury, he built a model town nearby for his employees. During both World Wars, Hershey's produced chocolate ration bars for American soldiers, making more than a billion of them during World War II. The Hershey's Company is today the leading North American manufacturer of chocolate confectioneries.

The process of making chocolate

The making of chocolate is labour-intensive. Cacao trees produce their first crops three to five years after being planted. Harvested twice a year, ripe cacao pods range in colour from red to green, yellow and purple. Harvesters use machetes or sharp knives to hack the pods from the trees and cut them open, revealing the seeds that are encased in a sweet white pulp. Both seeds and pulp are scooped out and usually left to ferment for a period of about a week, generally at or near the cacao farm.

Wild yeasts in the air convert the sugars in the pulp to alcohol, breaking the seeds down, activating enzymes and helping to develop the flavour. The highest quality chocolate is always made from properly fermented beans. The seeds must then be dried, usually on racks in the sun. Cacao brokers or, increasingly, artisan chocolate company buyers themselves, select and purchase single-estate beans or mixes of beans, which are bagged and shipped to chocolate companies throughout the world.

Left Cadbury was the first chocolate manufacturer to sell boxes of chocolates in the late 19th century.

Right Nestlé was the dominant chocolate-maker in the 19th century, as well as being the first to make milk chocolate.

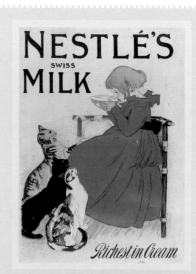

Above Milton Hershey created the leading American chocolate brand.

Above Artisan chocolatiers craft a variety of wonderful chocolates.

Home-made chocolates

With so many chocolate companies and so many unique and delicious chocolate products being made today, why make chocolates at home? Admittedly, it is a bit of a challenge. Attention to timing and temperature can mean the difference between a successful confection and one that fails. Good-quality (sometimes pricey) ingredients are also essential, and it is vital that recipes are followed carefully.

The primary motivating factor is the satisfaction that is to be gained by creating perfect little chocolate cups that will be filled with the first raspberries of the season, or the gooey chocolatey flavour of a flourless chocolate cupcake, which tastes infinitely better than any store-bought variety. A home-made plate of chocolate truffles flavoured with praline filling or scented with jasmine tea makes a statement that even the fanciest box of store-bought chocolate confections cannot.

Filling your kitchen with the irresistible smell of cooking chocolate, learning what works and what doesn't work, beginning to notice the chemistry of change, and finally tasting the fruits of your labour is definitely worth the time and money. As Milton Hershey said, "Chocolate is a permanent thing", and goes on giving pleasure to people of all ages around the world.

Having reached the factories, seeds are roasted, then shelled and winnowed to separate out the nibs, which are the essence of chocolate. The nibs are crushed into chocolate mass or liquor (a paste that contains no alcohol), and additional pressure is applied to separate out the cocoa butter. The remaining solids are pulverized into cocoa powder.

Manufacturers combine chocolate liquor, cocoa butter and cocoa powder in various ways along with sugar and/or milk to create different kinds of chocolate. The mixture is then smoothed by rotating blades in a process called conching, which removes moisture and volatile acids. The last step is to temper the chocolate to the desired consistency, texture and glossiness.

Artisan chocolates

Despite the huge range of mass-market, commercially produced chocolate bars available, there is a growing interest in artisan products made by an innovative generation of chocolatiers who treat chocolate production as an art form. Of course, this is nothing new. Before chocolate companies became international conglomerates, chocolate was always made by hand in small quantities. Now artisan chocolate manufacturers are creating unique types of chocolate and chocolate confections in small batches once again, often using antique equipment. They craft chocolate in the way a knowledgeable vintner crafts a fine wine or a passionate coffee roaster creates a unique blend – with attention to detail, respect for the ingredients and a search for something special.

Chocolate and Easter

For centuries eggs have been associated with the Christian holiday, Easter. A pagan symbol adopted by early Christians, the egg symbolizes new life and rebirth. The modern custom of chocolate eggs has joined the tradition of decorating hen's eggs. Easter egg hunts, where chocolate eggs are hidden for children to search out, are a popular activity.

Sweet-making ingredients

The biggest advantage to making sweets and chocolates at home is that you, as the cook, have complete control over the ingredients, and there is such a tempting choice to be found. The majority of the ingredients called for in this book can easily be purchased from most local stores (or may even be in your storecupboard already), although a few will need to come from a speciality store or be ordered on-line. It is certainly worth the effort of seeking out these lesser-known ingredients, as the array of confections that can be made is almost endless.

Sugar

As it comes in many different varieties, you need to make sure you pick the right type of sugar for your recipe. **Icing (confectioners') sugar** is the best type to use when a very fine texture is needed, while **caster (superfine) sugar** is used for baking confections and sponges. **Granulated (white) sugar** has a chunkier texture than caster sugar, and **preserving sugar**, sometimes called lump sugar, is even more coarse and will yield a beautiful clear syrup for candying fruits or making fruit pastes and jellies. **Organic sugar** is always less refined, with a pale brown colour and a slightly richer flavour. Brown sugars vary from **demerara (raw) sugar**, which lends a deeper tint and texture to sweets, to **soft light** or **dark brown sugar**, which contains molasses to keep it soft.

Other sweeteners

Black treacle (molasses) is packed with iron and other minerals, and has a delicious flavour, which forms an integral part of shiny black liquorice. **Golden (light corn) syrup** is a beautiful colour, with a distinctive flavour. The bland taste of **liquid glucose (clear corn syrup)** is sometimes called for when golden syrup might overwhelm a delicate sweet.

Honey can range widely in flavour from light and sweet to dark and earthy, the flavour notes being dictated by the flowers that the bees pollinate. Lavender and heather honeys are more delicate and mild, whereas mountain and chestnut honeys are intensely flavoured.

Maple syrup is an expensive sweetener made by collecting the sap of the maple tree and then removing the water to reduce the sap into a syrup. Nothing is added, and nothing is removed except the water element. Used sparingly, it is worth the investment – it has a flavour like nothing else.

Above Rich-tasting full-fat milk is used to make creamy and smooth fudge and tablet, among other sweets.

Milk and cream

Full-fat (whole) milk is always the first choice for sweets and cakes because the high fat content will result in a smooth texture and rich taste. **Evaporated milk** has a unique and old-fashioned flavour that is especially good in fudge recipes, whereas **sweetened condensed milk** already includes a substantial amount of sugar and works well in liquorice.

Single (light) cream can be used in place of whole milk, but cannot be a substitute for **double (heavy) cream** in sweet-making, for example in creamy, tempting fudge or chocolate ganache.

Above Dark brown sugar has a soft texture and rich taste due to the molasses that it contains.

Above Golden syrup is sticky, viscous and extremely sweet, and has a pretty golden colour.

Fats

The best **butter** to use is an unsalted, high butterfat variety. As with double (heavy) cream, the higher the fat content, the lower the water content and the better the end result. Oils used in sweet-making should be as bland and flavourless as possible. **Grapeseed** is the best choice, followed by **peanut (groundnut)** or **almond oil**.

Eggs

The eggs you buy should be free range if available, and really fresh. If your eggs are kept in the refrigerator, warm them gently, in their shells, in lukewarm water before using. When whisking egg whites, always make sure that the bowl is clean and dry.

Flour

Plain (all-purpose) white flour is a finely milled flour made from soft wheat grain. It is ideal for making fragile pastry shells for

Above Gelatine is used to make sweets with a chewy texture, such as jellies.

delicate chocolate boats, as well as in recipes for classic chocolate brownies and tuiles. **Self-raising (self-rising) flour** is the same as plain flour but it has the addition of a raising agent, usually **bicarbonate of soda (baking soda)** and

cream of tartar. **American cake flour** is also a flour made with a soft wheat and sometimes an added raising agent. It is sifted many times.

Raising and thickening agents

Cream of tartar stabilizes and gives more volume to beaten egg whites so they do not separate (break) while they are being whisked to stiff peaks. **Baking powder** consists of bicarbonate of soda with an acid added to it, usually cream of tartar, and this helps cake and sweet mixtures to reach the correct volume when cooked.

Gelatine is a clear setting agent that helps give shape and brightness to jellies, marshmallows and gumdrops. It is an animal product so is not suitable for vegetarians, but there are also vegetarian alternatives available, which are derived from seaweed.

Fondant

A basic recipe of sugar and water, fondant is used in many sweet and chocolate recipes. Start the day before you need to use it.

1 Dampen a marble slab, a metal scraper and a wooden spatula with cold water. Prepare an ice-water bath.
2 Combine the sugar and water in a large, heavy pan and heat until the sugar dissolves. Bring to the boil, then lower the heat and cook until it reaches the soft-ball stage (114°C/238°F).
3 Arrest the cooking by placing the pan in the ice-water bath. Pour the syrup on to the prepared marble and leave it to cool for 3 minutes.
4 Using the damp metal scraper, begin to fold the edges into the centre of the pool until the mixture becomes glossy.

Makes about 400g/14oz

400g/14oz caster (superfine) sugar
150ml/ ½ pint/ ⅔ cup water

5 With the wooden spatula, work the syrup in a figure of eight movement for about 10 minutes, until the fondant is thick and opaque.
6 First with the metal scraper, and then with moist hands, work and knead the fondant for about 10 minutes to remove all lumps and create a smooth paste.
7 Lightly moisten a bowl with water and place the fondant inside. Cover the bowl with a damp, clean dish towel and leave the fondant to rest overnight (or for at least 12 hours) in the refrigerator.

Fruit

Large orchard fruits such as apples, pears and quinces are perfect for cooking down into concentrated pastes. Their dense textures and high natural pectin content mean they set well with the addition of a little sugar. **Smaller stone fruits** such as apricots and cherries have short seasons, but they are ideal for preserving as jellies or jams to be used later in the year. **Soft fruits** such as raspberries, blackberries and strawberries can be puréed into intense mixtures used for flavouring and colouring sweets or folding into whipped cream.

Citrus fruits add brightness and sparkle to many sweets and chocolates. Candied citrus peel is one of the most versatile ingredients in the sweet kitchen; the best types of fruit for this are organic oranges, mandarins or grapefruit, and all are delicious dipped in chocolate.

Fresh dates have tender flesh, encased in a papery skin, and are sweet and caramel-like in flavour. A little embellishment, such as stuffing with marzipan enlivened with grated orange rind, can make them very festive indeed. **Dried fruits** such as currants, sultanas (golden raisins), raisins, dried apricots, sour cherries and figs make appetizing additions to all kinds of sweets.

Nuts and seeds

All kinds of nuts work well in sweet recipes, from toasted or ground **almonds** (the base for all kinds of ancient sweet recipes) to **pecans**, **walnuts**, **macadamias** and vivid green **pistachios**. **Hazelnuts** make the quintessential praline, and should be toasted to bring out their flavour. **Sesame seeds** have great nutritional qualities and a lovely texture; they are a perfect match for honey. The delicate flavour of **pine nuts** adds depth and texture to cookies and brittles, while **peanuts** make a classic combination with chocolate or in peanut-flavoured popcorn.

Coconuts

These are neither a fruit nor a nut, but a huge seed. The flesh has a lovely texture and can be grated fresh or used dried to give texture and flavour to sweets. The oil is also used to give a silky texture to chocolate.

Flavourings

The most commonly used flavouring in sweets is **vanilla**. Each vanilla pod (bean) contains thousands of tiny seeds that lend both taste and texture to recipes. If you are using vanilla extract, buy a good quality one for the full flavour.

Above Peanuts are a very tasty, protein-packed base for many sweets and chocolates.

Rose water and **orange blossom water** should both be used sparingly, as they can overwhelm a delicate confection. The syrup form, such as **rose or violet syrup**, is already sweetened and more concentrated in flavour, so use less.

Alcohol used for cooking should always be good enough to drink. All kinds of liqueurs can be used in chocolate-making. Champagne is wonderful, but Italian prosecco, Spanish cava and some New World sparkling wines are less expensive and taste delicious too.

Coffee beans should be bought freshly roasted and whole if possible. The flavour is better if you grind your own beans as needed. **Dried spices** such as aniseeds do not last for ever either – buy some fresh ones and you will immediately notice the difference from their fabulously intense aroma.

A fine cooking or table **salt** is essential for mixing into a batter; however, when it comes to embellishment or when a more complex salty taste and a coarser texture is desired, there are many interesting varieties to choose from. A good salt complements liquorice, caramel and chocolate very well.

Above Fresh fruits, such as delicious clementines, can be made into candied citrus peel with just water and sugar.

Above Vanilla pods have a wonderful flavour, but if you can not buy them, you could use vanilla extract instead.

Decorations

At cake-decorating stores, **colourings** can be found in dizzying variations. Liquid colours are lower in concentration than pastes or gels, and you will have to use a lot more to get the desired shade; however, using too much liquid colour can taint the flavour of your sweets. **Powders** and **lustre dusts** are wonderful for creating texture and highlights. Use a soft paintbrush and tap it against your hand to drop sparkly sprinkles on to your sweets.

Gold and silver dust or **leaf** for cooking is found in speciality cake-decorating stores and art stores. The dust can also be mixed with clear unflavoured vodka and then painted on top of chocolates for a decadent finish.

Candy sprinkles and decorations come in many shapes and sizes, including **hundreds and thousands** (tiny rainbow-coloured sprinkles), **large sugar shapes**, and **silver and gold balls** (drageés). Monochromatic or metallic sprinkles give a sophisticated look.

Chocolate and cocoa

Along with unsweetened cocoa, chocolate should be the best quality you can find. Large blocks of chocolate for cooking are available at fine food stores and on-line, but it also comes in the form of beans, lozenges, pastilles or drops (chips). It needs to be chopped very finely for tempering.

When choosing chocolate for cooking, make sure you find the kind specified in the recipe. **Cooking (unsweetened)** chocolate is very bitter and is not suitable for eating on its own. **Dark (bittersweet) chocolate** is a combination of chocolate mass (at least 55 per cent), cocoa butter and sugar, while **plain (semisweet) chocolate** is generally made of 35 to 55 per cent chocolate mass. **Milk chocolate** has at least 12 per cent added milk or cream, and **white chocolate** is a combination of about 20 per cent cocoa butter, sugar and milk, with no chocolate mass at all.

Cocoa powder has a distinctively bitter taste on its own, but when mixed into cakes, biscuits (cookies) and sweets with sugar, it is transformed. It also makes a delicious topping when dusted lightly over cakes, cookies and truffles as an alternative to icing (confectioners') sugar.

Tempering chocolate

The process of tempering involves melting chocolate carefully to a certain temperature, cooling, then reheating it, so that the right kind of crystals predominate to give it a glossy, smooth finish.

Different types of chocolate need different temperatures (see chart). It is vital to use a chocolate thermometer, which records very low temperatures.

Type of chocolate	First melt to:	Then cool to:	Melt again to:
Dark (bittersweet)	40–45°C or 104–113°F	27–28°C or 80–82°F	31–32°C or 88–89°F
Milk	32.5°C or 90°F	27–28°C or 80–82°F	30°C or 86°F
White	30.5°C or 87°F	27°C or 80°F	28°C or 82°F

1 Take two-thirds of the chopped chocolate and put it into a heatproof bowl.
2 Place the bowl over a pan of barely simmering water, making sure no water or steam comes into contact with the chocolate. Use a chocolate thermometer to melt it according to the chart.
3 When the chocolate is almost melted, remove the bowl from the pan of simmering water and place it on a kitchen towel.
4 Use a wooden spoon to stir the chocolate gently. Add the remaining chocolate a little at a time until the pieces cease to melt.
5 Allow the chocolate to continue to cool down on its own according to the chart (this should take 10–15 minutes).
6 Bring it back up to the third temperature on the chart by placing the bowl back over the pan.
7 Now follow the recipe instructions.

Sweet-making equipment

It is an undeniable fact that a few essential pieces of equipment will make sweet- and chocolate-making at home a much easier process. You will probably have many of these items in your kitchen already, and may only need to invest in a couple of extra items, such as a copper pan and a good sugar thermometer, to get started. The following pages give descriptions of the most useful tools you will need, from basic kitchen cooking equipment, such as ladles and spatulas, to specialist tools for intricate sweet-decorating, such as paint brushes and dipping forks.

Large equipment

A good quality, unlined, solid **copper pan** with a heavy base is always worth the money. The copper stands up well to the high temperatures used in sweet-making.

A marble slab is very useful for making fondants, boiled sweets and taffies.

Cake tins (pans) of all shapes and sizes are indispensable in sweet-making. Small individual decorative **metal moulds** can be very useful for petit fours or for making decorative patterns on sweets. Stainless steel is best, but any heavy metal will do.

A collection of **heatproof bowls** in varying sizes is practical for melting chocolate and for many other mixing processes, and when the cooking is finished, a **cooling rack** will be very useful. The best racks have a crosshatch pattern, making them perfect for supporting miniature confections.

Small equipment

Ladles, spatulas and spoons are vital pieces of equipment. A **ladle** will help in delicate operations such as pouring chocolate into moulds or transferring liquids into jars. **Rubber spatulas** work brilliantly for scraping mixtures out of bowls, but **wooden spatulas** or **spoons** are best for stirring hot syrup and nut brittle, as they do not conduct the heat.

Above A balloon whisk is useful in chocolate-making, especially for those recipes that contain cream or egg whites.

A wire **balloon whisk** is ideal for whipping small amounts of cream by hand or mixing chocolate as it melts. A fine-mesh **sieve (strainer)** is vital for straining flavourings or for sifting dry ingredients such as icing (confectioners') sugar and flour.

Glass and plastic **measuring cups and jugs** for liquid are essential, while sturdy metal, ceramic or plastic **measuring spoons** are needed for adding small quantities of ingredients. A **ruler** helps the home cook to mark the size of truffles, pastes and fudges accurately before cutting for a professional-looking result.

Cutting tools

A heavy, solid, sharp **chef's knife** is the most practical implement for chopping hard ingredients such as chocolate and

Above A lot of equipment is needed for sweet- and chocolate-making, but much of it, for example measuring jugs and cake tins, may already be in your kitchen cupboards.

Boiled Sweets, Lollipops, Pulled Taffies and Fondants

Everyone has their favourite boiled sweet or pulled taffy, and whether you suck them slowly or crunch them up, they provide a satisfying taste experience. Made with sugar syrup and a variety of other ingredients, they require a bit of effort to make, but the results are well worth it. Easier on the arms, fondants are made using a slightly different process, and this gives them a softer, more chewy texture. All types can be made in many flavours and colours, so get creative!

Sweet, suckable and sticky

Boiled sweets, pulled taffies, lollipops and fondants all start with the simple combination of sugar and water, which is made into a syrup, heated to a specific temperature and treated in various ways to create different textures.

For simple hard-boiled sweets (candies), such as Pear Drops, or lollipops, the syrup is taken to the hard-crack stage, flavoured and poured either into a mould or on to an oiled surface to set. For lollipops, a stick is pushed into setting pools of syrup until they cool and harden.

For other types, the syrup can be handled in various ways as it cools to get dramatically different results. Manipulating a syrup that has been taken to the hard-crack stage by pulling and stretching it adds hundreds of tiny air bubbles to the syrup, making the mixture lighter in colour and texture. Many of the sweets in this chapter are made in this way, varied primarily by the addition of different flavourings and colourings, and, in the case of Rhubarb and Custards and Peppermint Humbugs, by combining two flavours and colours together.

Over-stretching can cause the sweets to crumble or become too grainy, so following these recipes carefully is very important if you want to achieve the desired result. The pulling and stretching process requires a bit of hard work, but once you have mastered the technique you will be able to create home-made versions of many store-bought sweets by experimenting with flavours.

Softer, chewier Edinburgh Rock and Salt-water Taffy, although made using a similar stretching technique, are based on a sugar syrup that has been taken to a different stage during the heating process, meaning they don't set as hard. Exposing the rock to air for 24 hours means that the sweets become even softer and crumblier.

Fondants are softer still and, unlike pulled sweets, getting a grain into the syrup is exactly the object as it is this that produces the desired texture. Once made, a basic fondant can be flavoured and shaped into balls or melted down and poured into decorative paper cups to set, as well as being used as the centre for a huge range of different chocolates.

Pear drops

These simple drops look especially lovely when poured into an antique mould to make little nuggets. Otherwise, pour them out free-form on to an oiled marble slab or baking sheet. They are a traditional favourite in many countries, and jars of them are still common in old-fashioned sweet shops.

1 Grease a mould, baking sheet or marble slab with the oil. Set aside a large bowl full of cold water or fill the sink with a little water.

2 Put the sugar, 50ml/2fl oz/¼ cup water, 150ml/¼ pint/⅔ cup pear juice and cream of tartar in a heavy pan. Heat over a moderate heat until the sugar has dissolved.

3 Increase the heat and boil the mixture until it reaches the soft-ball stage (114°C/238°F).

4 Add the lime juice, the remaining pear juice and the food colouring. Resist the temptation to stir as this could cause the syrup to crystallize.

5 Bring back to the boil and cook until it reaches the hard-crack stage (154°C/310°F).

6 Remove from the heat and place over the cold water to arrest the cooking.

7 Spoon immediately into the greased mould or drop spoonfuls on to the baking sheet or marble slab.

8 Allow to cool completely before removing from the mould or surface using the tip of a knife or an offset spatula.

9 Serve immediately, or wrap in baking parchment or waxed paper and store in an airtight container.

VARIATION: To make candy shards, pour the syrup into an oiled Swiss roll tin (jelly roll pan) and leave to set. Once it is hard, drop the tray on the counter or floor to shatter it, and remove the pieces with a knife.

makes: about 600g/1lb 6oz

grapeseed or groundnut (peanut) oil, for greasing

450g/1lb/2¼ cups caster (superfine) sugar

175ml/6fl oz/¾ cup pear juice

1.25ml/¼ tsp cream of tartar

30ml/2 tbsp lime juice

1 drop green food colouring

makes: about 675g/1½lb

grapeseed or groundnut (peanut) oil, for greasing

300g/11oz raspberries

400g/14oz/2 cups caster (superfine) sugar

Raspberry lollipops

Fruit juice lollipops are one of the best ways to preserve the natural flavour of perfectly ripe berries. These raspberry lollipops have a wonderful colour, and taste even better than they look. Experiment with different berries or fresh fruit juices to make a range of fun and delicious lollipops.

1 Grease a baking sheet with the oil and prepare an ice-water bath.

2 Put the raspberries in a heavy pan and heat gently until the fruits soften and the juices run. Do not stir.

3 Strain through a sieve (strainer) placed over a large bowl to catch the juices. Do not push the berries through the sieve as this will cause the juice to go cloudy.

4 Put the sugar in a heavy pan and add the strained raspberry juice. Stir the mixture over a medium heat until the sugar dissolves, then bring to the boil.

5 Stop stirring and boil over moderate heat until the syrup reaches the hard-crack stage (154°C/310°F).

6 Arrest the cooking by placing the pan in the ice-water bath.

7 Pour spoonfuls of the syrup on to the prepared baking sheet, about 5cm/2in apart. Press lollipop sticks into the syrup, then pour another drop of syrup over the top of the stick to seal it in.

8 Allow the lollipops to cool completely before lifting gently from the sheet and wrapping them individually in cellophane.

Jewelled lollipops

Iconic across the world, lollipops are always popular with children. They are often round or oval-shaped and come in many colours. These jewelled ones are a simple variation, using some dried fruit and nuts for texture and decoration

1 Grease a marble slab or heavy baking sheet. Prepare an ice-water bath.

2 Put the water into a large, heavy pan and cover it with the sugar and liquid glucose or cream of tartar.

3 Boil the syrup until it reaches the hard-crack stage (154°C/310°F). Remove the pan from the heat immediately.

4 Arrest the cooking by placing the pan in the ice-water bath.

5 Pour or spoon circles of syrup on to the greased surface, reserving about one-fifth of the syrup.

6 Press in the dried fruits and nuts to make a pleasing, random pattern.

7 Working quickly, press lollipop sticks or thin wooden dowels into each lollipop, then pour a drop of the remaining syrup over the top of each stick so that it is sealed in.

8 Leave the lollipops to harden for about 10 minutes, then remove them carefully from the surface by holding on to the stick. Go slowly; they will come up eventually. You may have some breakages, but the recipe makes plenty to account for this, and you can still eat the broken ones.

9 Serve immediately, or wrap in baking parchment or waxed paper and store for a few days in an airtight container.

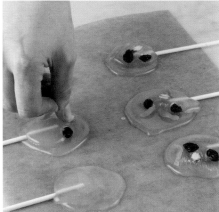

makes: about 12 lollipops

grapeseed or groundnut (peanut) oil, for greasing

100ml/3½fl oz/scant ½ cup water

400g/14oz/2 cups caster (superfine) sugar

15ml/1 tbsp liquid glucose or 5ml/1 tsp cream of tartar

40g/1½oz assorted dried fruits, such as cranberries, sultanas (golden raisins) and apricots

25g/1oz shelled pistachio nuts

makes: about 600g/1lb 6oz

grapeseed or groundnut (peanut) oil, for greasing

400g/14oz/2 cups caster (superfine) sugar

100ml/3½ fl oz/scant ½ cup liquid glucose or golden (light corn) syrup

100ml/3½ fl oz/scant ½ cup water

15ml/1 tbsp red food colouring or 3 drops concentrated colour paste or gel

15ml/1 tbsp pulverized anise seeds or 10ml/2 tsp anise extract

Cook's Tip

Twisted moulds are traditionally used for shaping these classic sweets, and may be found on-line or in specialist stores. The method given here provides a nice hand-made finish.

Aniseed twists

Also known as anise candy, these little hard sweets have a lovely depth of flavour. They can be made with anise extract, or you can infuse the twists with the flavour from fresh anise seeds, which imparts a stronger flavour.

1 Grease a marble slab, metal scraper and some scissors. Prepare an ice-water bath.

2 Combine the sugar, liquid glucose or golden syrup and water in a medium, heavy pan and bring to the boil.

3 Reduce the heat to medium and cook, without stirring, until the mixture reaches the soft-crack stage (143°C/290°F). Add the food colouring and anise seeds or extract.

4 Arrest the cooking by placing the pan in the ice-water bath.

5 Pour the sugar syrup on to the prepared marble and leave it to cool until a skin forms on the surface.

6 Using the oiled scraper, begin to fold the edges into the centre of the pool until it is cool enough to handle.

7 Oil your hands and, with the aid of the metal scraper, lift the syrup up off the marble and work it into a cylindrical shape. Pull it out from either end to make a long, thick strand.

8 Take hold of the ends of the syrup strand and pull them up towards you to form a 'U' shape.

9 Twist the two sides together into a rope shape. Continue to stretch the rope, twisting the whole time, until it is about 1cm/½ inch thick.

10 Working quickly, use the oiled scissors to cut the strand into even, bitesize pieces.

11 Wrap the aniseed twists in cellophane sweet wrappers. Serve immediately or store in an airtight container.

Lemon drops

Adorable miniature lemon-shaped drops are a classic sweet around the world. Opaque yellow with a sugary coating, they have a certain sparkle and should be put in beautiful little dishes to entice your family and friends to eat them. Lemon drops are also known as lemon sherbets.

makes: about 600g/1lb 6oz

grapeseed or groundnut (peanut) oil, for greasing

400g/14oz/2 cups caster (superfine) sugar

15ml/1 tbsp liquid glucose or golden (light corn) syrup

150ml/¼ pint/⅔ cup water

2.5ml/½ tsp lemon oil or 5ml/1 tsp lemon extract

2 drops yellow food colouring

200g/7oz/1 cup caster sugar, for dusting

Cook's Tip

Be sure to use a high-quality lemon extract or oil. Lemon extract is usually lemon oil diluted with water, so you will need to use more to get the strong lemony flavour.

1 Grease a marble slab, metal scraper and some kitchen scissors. Prepare an ice-water bath.

2 Combine the sugar, liquid glucose or golden syrup and water in a medium, heavy pan and bring to the boil.

3 Reduce the heat to medium and cook, without stirring, until the mixture reaches the soft-crack stage (143°C/290°F).

4 Remove the pan from the heat and stir in the lemon oil or extract and yellow food colouring. Stir until the mixture stops bubbling. Arrest the cooking by placing the pan in the ice-water bath.

5 Pour the syrup on to the oiled marble slab and allow it to cool until a skin forms. Using the oiled scraper, begin to fold the edges into the centre of the pool until it is cool enough to handle.

6 Oil your hands and, with the aid of the scraper, lift the syrup up off the marble and work it into a cylindrical shape. Pull it out from either end to make a long strand.

7 Take hold of the ends of the syrup strand and pull them up towards you to form a 'U' shape.

8 Twist the two sides together into a rope, then pull again from both ends to make the 'U' shape.

9 Repeat these steps for about 15–20 minutes, until the syrup rope becomes opaque and a lot lighter in colour. You need to keep working it constantly so that it remains supple. If it becomes too hard, you can put it in a cool oven for a few minutes until it softens enough to work with again.

10 Gently pull the syrup into a long, thin strand again, then fold it in half and then in half again so that you have four even lengths. Twist these up into an even rope and pull until the diameter is about 2cm/1in.

11 Use the oiled scissors to cut the pulled syrup into small, even pieces. Roll the pieces into little ovals between your oiled hands.

12 Pinch each end into a point to make them look like lemons. Place the caster sugar in a bowl and toss in the lemon drops to coat.

13 Serve immediately, or wrap in baking parchment or waxed paper and store in an airtight container.

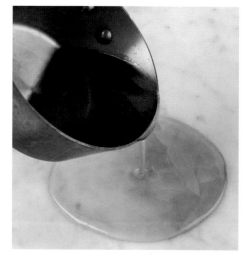
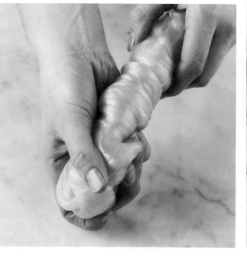

Rhubarb and custards

makes: about 600g/1lb 6oz

grapeseed or groundnut (peanut) oil, for greasing

450g/1lb/2¼ cups granulated (white) sugar, plus extra for tossing

150ml/¼ pint/⅔ cup water

1.5ml/¼ tsp cream of tartar

15ml/1 tbsp golden (corn) syrup

10ml/2 tsp tartaric acid

½ vanilla pod (bean), scraped

2–3 drops pink food colouring

Cook's Tip

Traditionally, these sweets are made without vanilla, comprising a plain, yellowish-white sweet on one side and a slightly tart pink one on the other, but the addition of fresh vanilla in this recipe perfectly balances the flavours and makes them more special. You could omit the vanilla if you prefer, or use 2 drops vanilla extract instead.

Inspired by a delicious dessert made from stewed rhubarb and vanilla-flavoured custard that was once common in schools and nurseries, these iconic two-tone treats are one of the most popular and enduring British boiled sweets.

1 Grease a marble slab, metal scraper and some scissors. Prepare an ice-water bath. Preheat the oven to 150°C/300°F/Gas 2.
2 Combine the sugar, water, cream of tartar and golden syrup in a medium, heavy pan and stir over a medium heat to dissolve the sugar. Bring to the boil.
3 Reduce the heat to medium and cook, without stirring, until it reaches the soft-crack stage (143°C/290°F). Add the tartaric acid and swirl the pan around. Place the pan in the ice-water bath for a few moments.
4 Pour the syrup on to the marble slab and leave it to cool until a skin forms. Using the oiled scraper, cut off half the syrup and place it back in the pan. Place the pan in the oven to prevent it from hardening.
5 Using the scraper, begin to fold the edges into the centre of the larger portion of syrup until it is cool enough to handle. Add the scraped vanilla seeds to the syrup.
6 Oil your hands and, with the aid of the scraper, lift the syrup up off the marble and work it into a cylindrical shape, mixing the vanilla seeds into the centre as you go. Pull it out from either end to make a long strand.

7 Take hold of the ends of the syrup strand and pull them up to form a 'U' shape. Twist the two sides together into a rope, then pull again from both ends to make the 'U' shape.
8 Repeat these steps for about 15–20 minutes, until the syrup rope becomes opaque and a lot lighter in colour. You need to keep working it constantly so that it remains supple. If it becomes too hard, you can put it in a cool oven for a few minutes until it softens enough to work with again.
9 Place the pulled vanilla-flavoured piece in the warm pan and set aside, removing the unpulled piece of syrup from the pan.
10 Working quickly, add the pink food colouring to the mixture and incorporate it by working the syrup with the scraper. Form it into a thick log.
11 Press the vanilla piece alongside the pink one. Pull the whole thing gently at both ends, pressing the two strands together, until it is the desired thickness. Leave to cool slightly.
12 Using oiled scissors, cut small, even pieces from the strand. Toss in the sugar.
13 Serve immediately or wrap in baking parchment and store in an airtight container.

Peppermint humbugs

makes: about 500g/1¼lb

grapeseed or groundnut (peanut) oil, for greasing

450g/1lb/2 ¼ cups granulated (white) sugar

150ml/¼ pint/⅔ cup water

1.5ml/¼ tsp cream of tartar

15ml/1 tbsp golden (corn) syrup

10ml/2 tsp peppermint extract

2–3 drops black food colouring

'Humbug', meaning a hoax or hypocrite, was a term used frequently in the 18th and 19th centuries, most famously by Charles Dickens in *A Christmas Carol*. The sweet was developed in England around the same time, and was perhaps given the name because of the unexpected intensity of the peppermint flavour which belies the appearance of the sweet. Traditionally a hard brown or black and white confection with a chewy centre, humbugs can now range in texture from minty toffees to hard sweets, as here.

1 Grease a marble slab, metal scraper and some kitchen scissors. Prepare an ice-water bath and preheat the oven to 150°C/300°F/Gas 2.

2 Combine the sugar, water, cream of tartar and golden syrup in a medium, heavy pan and bring to the boil.

3 Reduce the heat to medium and cook, without stirring, until it reaches the soft-crack stage (143°C/290°F). Add the peppermint oil.

4 Remove the pan from the heat and arrest the cooking by momentarily placing the base of the pan in the ice-water bath.

5 Pour the syrup on to the oiled marble slab and allow it to cool until a skin forms.

6 Using the oiled scraper, cut off one third of the syrup and place it back in the pan. Place the pan in the warm oven to prevent it from hardening while you work the rest of the syrup.

7 Using the oiled metal scraper, begin to fold the edges into the centre of the larger portion of syrup until it is cool enough to handle.

8 Oil your hands and, with the aid of the scraper, lift the syrup up off the marble and work it into a cylindrical shape. Pull it out from either end to make a long strand.

9 Take hold of the ends of the syrup strand and pull them up towards you to form a 'U' shape.

10 Twist the two sides together into a rope, then pull again from both ends to make the 'U' shape.

11 Repeat these steps for about 15–20 minutes, until the syrup rope becomes opaque and a lot lighter in colour. You need to keep working it constantly so that it remains supple. If it becomes too hard, you can put it in a cool oven for a few minutes until it softens enough to work with again.

12 Divide the pulled syrup into four sections using the scraper. Pull each of these out to form strands of an equal length and thickness.

13 Remove the un-pulled piece of syrup from the pan. Working quickly, add the black food colouring to the mixture and incorporate it by working the syrup with the scraper.

14 Shape the black mixture into a thick log that is about the same length as the white pieces. It should be quite a bit thicker than the white pieces.

15 Press the four white ropes of taffy alongside and into the black piece, spacing them evenly around the central black piece.

16 Pull the whole thing gently at both ends until the combined piece is the required thickness. Twist once or twice so the white strands spiral around the black.

17 If the humbug taffy is still a bit soft, leave it to cool slightly and firm up a bit more.

18 Using oiled scissors, cut small, even pieces from the strand.

19 Serve immediately, or wrap in baking parchment or waxed paper and store in an airtight container.

Rose water Edinburgh rock

Edinburgh rock was one of those cooking mishaps that turned into a triumph. It is not like conventional British rock. The story has it that some boiled sweets were exposed to air overnight and went soft and powdery. These can be made in any flavour, but the delicate subtlety of rose water works particularly well.

1 Grease a marble slab, metal pastry scraper and some kitchen scissors. Prepare an ice-water bath.

2 Combine the sugar, liquid glucose or golden syrup, cream of tartar and water in a medium, heavy pan. Heat gently over medium heat until the sugar dissolves.

3 Bring to the boil and boil the syrup until it reaches the soft-crack stage (143°C/290°F).

4 Stir in the colouring and rose water and immediately place the pan over the ice-water bath to arrest the cooking.

5 Pour the syrup on to the oiled marble slab and allow it to cool until a skin forms on the surface.

6 Using the oiled scraper, begin to fold the edges into the centre of the pool until it is cool enough to handle.

7 Dust your hands with icing sugar. Take hold of the ends of the syrup strand and pull them up towards you to form a 'U' shape. Press the two sides together and form it into the 'U' shape again. Do not twist the strands. Continue for 10 minutes until the mixture becomes opaque.

8 Pull it into a long strip, then cut it into small pieces with the oiled scissors.

9 Leave the rock out at room temperature for about 24 hours until it becomes soft and powdery. Serve immediately or store in an airtight container.

makes: about 675g/1½lb

grapeseed or groundnut (peanut) oil, for greasing

450g/1lb/2¼ cups granulated (white) sugar

15ml/1 tbsp liquid glucose or golden (light corn) syrup

2.5ml/½ tsp cream of tartar

200ml/7fl oz/scant 1 cup water

10ml/2 tsp pink food colouring, or 2 drops concentrated colour paste or gel

10ml/2 tsp rose water

icing (confectioners') sugar, for dusting

grapeseed or groundnut (peanut) oil,
for greasing

200g/7oz/1 cup caster (superfine) or
granulated (white) sugar

15ml/1 tbsp cornflour (cornstarch)

150ml/¼ pint/⅔ cup liquid glucose or
golden (light corn) syrup

25g/1oz unsalted butter

120ml/4fl oz/½ cup water

1.5ml/¼ tsp sea salt

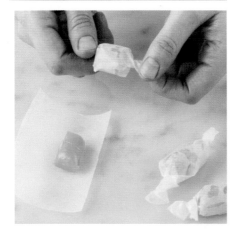

Salt-water taffy

Supposedly made with sea water, salt-water taffy is originally from Atlantic City,
although you used to be able to find it along the boardwalks at most American
seaside towns. Soft and chewy and with the addition of a pinch of salt, it's the
perfect treat. Chewing on these, you can almost hear the seagulls.

1 Grease a marble slab, metal pastry
scraper and some kitchen scissors.
2 Combine the sugar and cornflour in a
large, heavy pan. Add the liquid glucose or
golden syrup, butter, water and salt and
cook over moderate heat until the mixture
reaches the soft-ball stage (114°C/238°F).
3 Remove the pan from the heat and
pour it on to the prepared marble slab.
Leave to cool for a few minutes, until the
taffy can be handled comfortably.
4 Oil your hands and, with the aid of the
scraper, lift the syrup up off the marble and
work it into a cylindrical shape. Pull it out
from either end to make a long, thick strand.
5 Take hold of the ends of the syrup
strand and pull them up towards you to
form a 'U' shape.

6 Twist the two sides together into a rope
shape. Continue to stretch the rope
(twisting the whole time) until it is lighter
and firm enough to hold a shape. This may
take 10 minutes.
7 Stretch the strand until it is 2½cm/1in
in diameter. Using the oiled scissors, snip
into bitesize pieces.
8 Wrap each piece of taffy individually in
squares of waxed paper, twisting the ends
to seal. Serve immediately, or store in an
airtight container.

VARIATION: You could add food colouring
and different flavours, such as orange, to
the syrup just as it reaches the hard-ball
stage. Traditionally, salt-water taffy comes
in pastel shades.

Lemon cream dreams

Soft, lemony, chewy morsels, these are wonderful sweets for sunny afternoons. They can be served alongside scones at a tea party or alternatively, you can dress them down by wrapping the cooled, set sweets in little squares of parchment paper to take on picnics. Start the day before you need them.

makes: 25–30 mini sweets

400g/14oz/2 cups caster (superfine) sugar

150ml/½ pint/⅔ cup water

45–60ml/3–4 tbsp lemon juice

zest of 1 lemon

50g/2oz candied lemon peel, chopped

25g/2oz pistachios, chopped

1 Dampen a marble slab, a metal scraper and a wooden spatula with cold water. Prepare an ice-water bath.

2 Combine the sugar and water in a large, heavy pan and heat until the sugar dissolves. Bring to the boil, then lower the heat and cook until it reaches the soft-ball stage (114°C/238°F).

3 Arrest the cooking by placing the pan in the ice-water bath. Pour the syrup on to the marble and leave it to cool for 3 minutes

4 Using the damp metal scraper, begin to fold the edges into the centre of the pool until the mixture becomes glossy.

5 With the wooden spatula, work the syrup in a figure of eight movement for about 10 minutes, until it is thick and opaque.

6 First with the scraper and then with moist hands, work and knead the fondant for 10 minutes to create a smooth paste.

7 Lightly moisten a bowl. Place the fondant inside and cover with a damp, clean dish towel. Leave to rest for at least 12 hours in the refrigerator.

8 Set out about 25–30 mini paper cases on a baking sheet.

9 Scoop the fondant into a heatproof bowl. Place over a pan of barely simmering water. The water in the pan should reach the same level as the fondant in the bowl.

10 Very carefully heat until just melted. If you take it too far, the fondant will go clear and then never set. Add the lemon juice and zest and stir to combine.

11 Pour the fondant into the paper cases and sprinkle with the chopped candied lemon peel and chopped pistachios.

12 Leave to cool at room temperature, then serve. They can be stored in an airtight container for a few days.

Fruit sherbet

Kids love fizzy sherbet, and it is easy to make at home. You could recreate a childhood classic by making lollipops to dip in the powder, a combination that evokes nostalgia on both sides of the Atlantic, as packets of such treats have long been a favourite both in the UK and the US.

1 Put the sugar into a food processor or blender and process or blend until the sugar is as fine as it possibly can be. This should take a few minutes.

2 Transfer to a bowl and add the tartaric or citric acid, lemon or orange extract and the food colouring, if using. Mix well.

3 Leave the powder to dry competely, preferably for a few hours, before storing in an airtight container.

4 Use the sherbet for dipping lollipops into or put a couple of teaspoons into a glass of ice water and stir, for a refreshing summer drink.

makes: 500g/1¼lb

500g/1¼lb/2½ cups caster (superfine) sugar

15ml/1 tbsp tartaric acid or citric acid

10–12 drops lemon or orange extract

1–2 drops colouring (optional)

Cook's Tip
To make a drink, simply combine a little powder with some water.

TOFFEES, CARAMELS AND NUT BRITTLES

An amazing range of textures can be achieved when sugar is combined with other ingredients, such as butter, cream and golden syrup, and heated to a specific temperature. From chewy toffees, firmer butterscotch, light-as-air honeycomb and crunchy nut brittles, there is sure to be something for everyone. Delicious on their own, these can be further enhanced by the addition of chocolate, nuts or seeds, or embellished with gold leaf for an extra-special touch.

Crunchy, chewy and buttery

While the base of the sweets in this chapter is sugar, the addition of other ingredients changes them into an entirely different indulgence. Lavish amounts of butter, cream or nuts added to an almost burnt sugar syrup result in a variety of toffees, caramels and nut brittles.

For toffees, sugar is boiled with water to the desired colour, then butter or cream is added. The longer cooking time of the sugar syrup means that toffees are harder than caramels, and they can be broken into pieces and sucked. The English favourite, Bonfire Toffee, devoured every year on 5 November, is darkened with black treacle (molasses) to resemble the dregs of a bonfire. Other toffees have baking soda added to them to lighten the texture. Honeycomb and cinder toffee are filled with little air bubbles created by this ingredient.

For soft caramels, the sugar is boiled with cream, which caramelizes at a lower temperature and is responsible for the chewy texture. Gently stirring the cooking mixture will help prevent the milk proteins from burning. Once soft caramels are poured and set, it is easy to cut them into pieces. They will keep well and be easiest to manage if they are wrapped in individual foils or squares of baking parchment. Caramel makes the perfect base for a range of flavourings, such as salt or chopped nuts, as well as coconut and fruits, such as clementines and apples. Caramel apples, or toffee apples as they are known in England, are an autumnal must.

Butterscotch is made in a similar way to caramel, but with added butter, as the name suggests.

Nut-packed brittles are more about the nuts than the caramel with regards to flavour, but it is the caramel that holds it all together. Mounds of nuts are added to a cooked sugar syrup and stirred gently. The mixture is then poured out on to an oiled surface, such as a marble slab, and allowed to cool. When cool enough to handle, the edges are pulled apart to make lacy pieces of brittle that are easily broken into shards. Some recipes add a little baking soda as well for an even lighter brittle.

200g/7oz macadamia nut halves, roughly chopped

60ml/4 tbsp water

350g/12oz/1¾ cups caster (superfine) sugar

125g/4¼oz unsalted butter

15ml/1 tbsp black treacle (molasses)

1.5ml/¼ tsp sea salt

5ml/1 tsp vanilla extract

1.5ml/¼ tsp bicarbonate of soda (baking soda)

150g/5oz dark (bittersweet) chocolate (60–70% cocoa solids), finely chopped

Nutty chocolate toffee

This toffee is crunchy and buttery and could be made with any of your favourite nuts. The combination of dark chocolate and macadamia works wonderfully, but pecans or hazelnuts would be delicious as well.

1 Preheat the oven to 160°C/325°F/Gas 3. Spread the macadamias out on a baking sheet and place in the oven.

2 Set a timer for 5 minutes and then check the nuts, giving them a toss. They may need another few minutes. They should be slightly golden but not brown. Because macadamia nuts contain a lot of oil they can burn easily, so keep an eye on them.

3 Line a shallow baking tray with baking parchment. Spread three-quarters of the macadamias out on the sheet, tightly packing them in a single layer. Reserve the rest for the topping.

4 Put the water, sugar, butter, black treacle and salt in a heavy pan. Place over a low heat and heat until everything is dissolved.

5 Bring to the boil and heat until the syrup reaches the hard-crack stage (154°C/310°F).

6 Immediately remove from the heat and stir in the vanilla extract and bicarbonate of soda. Stir thoroughly to incorporate the soda and vanilla, but do not overmix.

7 Quickly pour the mixture over the nuts. Shake the baking sheet and tap it on the counter so the surface is even.

8 Sprinkle the surface with the chocolate (which will melt into the toffee), then sprinkle with the remaining nuts.

9 Leave to cool completely, then break into pieces and serve. Store in an airtight container. Do not place in the refrigerator or freezer.

Pecan toffees

This recipe originally comes from New Orleans. Its French-Creole name is La Colle, which means 'glue', because when made correctly, it should have a thick and very smooth texture, interspersed with crunchy nuts.

1 Preheat the oven to 160°C/325°F/Gas 3. Spread the pecans out on a baking sheet and place in the oven.
2 Set a timer for 7 minutes and then check the nuts, giving them a toss. They will probably need another few minutes. Test whether they are done by breaking one in half. It should be slightly golden but not brown. You will just start to smell them when they are ready.
3 Remove the nuts from the oven and allow them to cool for a few minutes.
4 Chop the pecans roughly, then sift them to separate the fine powder from the nut pieces. Save the nut powder and set them both aside.

5 Put the water into a heavy pan and cover with the soft dark brown sugar. On low heat, dissolve the sugar completely.
6 Once the sugar has dissolved, turn the heat up to medium-high and bring the mixture to a boil until it reaches the soft-crack stage (143°C/290°F).
7 Stir in the toasted, chopped pecans.
8 Pour the mixture into paper cases, then sprinkle with the fine nut powder and leave to cool completely before serving. Store in an airtight container.

VARIATION: You can substitute the soft dark brown sugar with black treacle (molasses), but only use 225g/8oz/⅔ cup.

makes: about 550g/1lb 5 oz

125g/4¼oz pecans

50ml/2fl oz/¼ cup water

425g/15oz/scant 2 cups soft dark brown sugar

Cook's Tip
Stir the pecans in swiftly as the mixture will begin to set very quickly.

Cinder toffee

Like little golden cinders from the fire, this toffee is an old favourite in many parts of the world. It is known by lots of names, including yellow man, puff candy, hokey pokey, sponge candy, sea foam and angel food candy.

1   Prepare an ice-water bath. Grease a shallow baking tray and set aside.
2   Put the water in heavy pan and cover with the sugar and golden syrup.
3   Heat gently until the sugar dissolves. Increase the heat and bring to the boil without stirring until the syrup reaches just over the hard-crack stage (154°C/310°F) and begins to take on a little colour.
4   Remove the syrup from the heat and arrest the cooking by placing it over the ice-water bath for a moment.
5   Dissolve the bicarbonate of soda in the warm water.

6   Pour the bicarbonate of soda into the sugar syrup. At this point, it should bubble and froth up, so take great care.
7   Stir the mixture to disperse the bubbles throughout, working quickly, before pouring into the prepared baking sheet.
8   When cooled, break into pieces. Wrap the shards in cellophane, baking parchment or wax paper. Store in an airtight container.

VARIATION: For a really decadent treat you can dip toffee pieces in melted chocolate and allow them to set before eating.

makes: about 300g/11oz

butter, for greasing

60ml/4 tbsp water

225g/8oz/generous 1 cup caster (superfine) sugar

15ml/1 tbsp golden (light corn) syrup

1.5ml/¼ tsp bicarbonate of soda (baking soda), sifted

5ml/1 tsp warm water

makes: about 750g/1lb 13oz

- 125g/4¼oz unsalted butter, plus extra for greasing
- 30ml/2 tbsp cider vinegar or white wine vinegar
- 100ml/3½fl oz/scant ½ cup black treacle (molasses)
- 200ml/7fl oz/scant 1 cup golden (light corn) syrup
- 400g/14oz demerara (raw) sugar
- 2.5ml/½ tsp bicarbonate of soda (baking soda), sifted

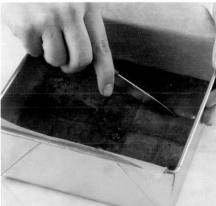

Honeycomb toffee

This recipe is a richer, more traditional version of honeycomb than Cinder Toffee. To make it lighter in colour and taste, and to update the flavour a little, replace the black treacle or molasses with more golden syrup.

1 Grease a 20cm/8in square cake tin (pan). Line it with a sheet of baking parchment so that each end of the paper comes up the sides of the tin. This will make it easier to remove the honeycomb.

2 Melt the butter gently in a large, heavy pan over a low heat. Add the vinegar, molasses, golden syrup and demerara sugar. Stir gently until the sugar has dissolved into the butter.

3 Turn the heat up to medium then, without stirring, heat the syrup until it reaches the hard-crack stage (154°C/310°F).

4 Remove the pan from the heat and immediately stir in the sifted bicarbonate of soda. As the mixture begins to froth, stir it once again. Take great care as the hot syrup bubbles up.

5 Pour the mixture into the prepared tin and leave it to cool. When it begins to set (after about 30 minutes), score the toffee with a knife into bitesize pieces.

6 Leave it to cool completely for a few hours before taking hold of the sides of the paper and lifting the block out of the tin. Break or cut into squares or rectangles. Store in an airtight container.

makes about 600g/1lb 6oz

125g/4¼oz unsalted butter, plus extra for greasing

225ml/7.5fl oz/scant 1 cup black treacle (molasses)

200g/7oz/scant 1 cup demerara (raw) sugar

tiny pinch of salt

Cook's Tip

If you pour the toffee into a smaller, deeper baking tray it will have a chewier texture.

Bonfire toffee

Dark, intensely flavoured and satisfyingly hard and brittle to crunch on, this traditional British toffee is the perfect accompaniment to fireworks and fun on Bonfire Night. The dark shards taste strongly of black treacle, but this is rounded by the demerara sugar and the richness of the butter.

1 Grease a shallow baking tray.

2 Melt the butter in a large, heavy pan over a low heat.

3 Add the black treacle, the demerara sugar and salt, and let them gently dissolve into the butter.

4 Once they have dissolved, turn the heat up to medium and bring to the boil.

5 Boil until the mixture is just below the hard-crack stage (154°C/310°F).

6 Pour the syrup into the prepared baking sheet and leave it to cool for about 10 minutes.

7 When it is cold, break into shards. Wrap individually in baking parchment and store in an airtight container.

Burnt caramel shards

makes: about 400g/14oz

100g/3¾oz unsalted butter, plus extra for greasing

300g/11oz/1½ cups caster (superfine) sugar

2 sheets of edible gold leaf (optional)

A very different method for making toffee, this recipe does not require a sugar thermometer. Gold leaf is expensive but it makes the caramel shards look really beautiful. You could bash up the caramel to make a crunchy ice cream topping, in which case, do not apply the gold leaf.

1 Grease a baking tray with butter and set it aside.

2 Melt the butter gently in a heavy pan. Add the sugar and stir constantly until the mixture is a dark caramel colour. This may take 10 minutes. The sugar and butter may separate during the cooking, but should come back together again in an emulsified mass by the time the mixture is the right colour.

3 Pour the syrup on to the prepared tray and leave to cool for about 30 minutes.

4 Apply the gold leaf (if using) to the surface of the caramel once it has cooled completely. *See* Cook's Tip.

5 Break into slim shards. Serve immediately or store in an airtight container. If you want to use it as a topping, put the caramel between two sheets of baking parchment and bash with a hammer into small pieces.

Cook's Tip

Gold leaf can come in two different formats: loose leaf or pressed to paper. The type that is pressed to paper must be rubbed off by inverting the paper on to the surface that is to have the gold leaf on it. Using your finger, rub the back of the paper firmly and lift it away. The gold leaf should be securely affixed to the surface. If you use loose leaf gold, use a clean, dry paint or pastry brush to lift it from between the sheets of paper that hold it and lower it on to the surface you want to cover with the gold.

Salted caramels

These dark caramels have a wonderful little crunch of sea salt. Although it may be a surprising addition to a confection, the salt cuts the sweetness of the caramel and creates a lovely balance.

1 Line a 23cm/9in square cake tin (pan) with baking parchment so that the paper comes up the sides of the tin on all sides.
2 Gently heat the cream in a heavy pan. Scrape the seeds from the vanilla pod and add them and the pod to the pan.
3 Bring the cream to just under a boil, being careful not to scorch it. When it is ready, it will start to exude wisps of steam and have a thin layer of frothy foam beginning to form at the edges of the pan.
4 While the cream is heating, heat the golden syrup or sugar in another heavy pan until it reaches the hard-crack stage (154°C/310°F).

5 Add the butter and 5ml/1 tsp salt, then strain the cream mixture into the sugar mixture. Stir to combine only, then bring the whole mixture back up to the firm-ball stage (120°C/248°F).
6 Pour the caramel into the prepared tin. Discard the vanilla pod. Tamp down the caramel mixture to release any air bubbles. Sprinkle with the remaining salt.
7 Leave to cool completely for a few hours before taking hold of the sides of the paper and lifting the caramel block out of the tin. Cut into squares or rectangles.
8 Wrap individually in foils and store in an airtight container at room temperature.

makes: about 1.15 kg/1lb 9oz

450ml/¾ pint/scant 2 cups double (heavy) cream

1 vanilla pod (bean), split down the side

225g/8oz golden (light corn) syrup

400g/14oz/2 cups caster (superfine) or granulated (white) sugar

65g/2½oz unsalted butter

7.5ml/1½ tsp fleur de sel or other fine sea salt

Cook's Tips
* You could decorate the surface with sheets of gold or silver leaf.
* You can also fill individual sweet cases with the caramel mixture when it is hot. You must only use unlined foil cases as the paper ones will stick to the caramel.

Fresh coconut and cardamom caramels

The texture of fresh coconut suspended in chewy caramel is a lovely surprise, while the distinct flavour of the cardamom cuts through the sweetness. The rum adds the finishing touch, making these a tropical taste sensation!

makes: about 1kg/2¼lb

freshly grated flesh of 1 coconut

500g/1¼lb/2½ cups caster (superfine) sugar

200ml/7fl oz/scant 1 cup golden (light corn) syrup

225ml/7.5fl oz/scant 1 cup double (heavy) cream

50g/2oz unsalted butter, cut into cubes, plus extra for greasing

1.5ml/¼ tsp ground cardamom

10ml/2 tsp white rum

1 Butter and line a 20 x 30cm/8 x 12in square baking tin (pan) with baking parchment or waxed paper.

2 Heat a large, heavy pan and drop the grated coconut into it, stirring constantly until the coconut is dry and flaky. You may need to do this in several batches. Put the coconut into a bowl and set aside.

3 Put the sugar, golden syrup and cream in a clean, heavy pan over moderate heat and stir constantly to dissolve the sugar and combine the ingredients. Add the butter, cardamom and coconut.

4 When the butter is melted, bring the pan to the boil and, without stirring, let the mixture go at a slow rolling boil for about 10 minutes, or until it reaches the soft-ball stage (114°C/238°F).

5 Remove the pan from the heat and stir in the rum. Pour the mixture into the prepared tin and leave to cool completely. This can take up to eight hours.

6 Cut into squares and wrap in waxed paper or foil wrappers. Store in an airtight container at room temperature. They will keep for about 10 days.

Caramel-pecan chews

These extra-dark caramels are silky and chewy with an added crunch of pecans. They are almost like a bitesize pecan pie without the pastry. Pecans are native to the southern United States and make a natural pairing with caramelized sugar.

makes: about 48 caramels

450ml/¾ pint/scant 2 cups double (heavy) cream

1 vanilla pod (bean), split down the side

225g/8oz golden (light corn) syrup

400g/14oz/2 cups granulated (white) sugar

65g/2½oz unsalted butter

5ml/1 tsp fluer de sel or other fine sea salt

100g/3¾oz toasted, chopped pecans

edible gold leaf (optional)

Cook's Tip
It is best to use unlined foil cases as they are less likely to stick.

1 Arrange 48 mini foil sweet cases on one or two baking trays and set aside.
2 Gently heat the cream in a heavy pan. Scrape the seeds from the vanilla pod and add them and the pod to the cream.
3 Bring the cream and vanilla to just under a boil, being careful not to scorch it. When it is ready, it will start to exude wisps of steam and have a thin layer of frothy foam beginning to form at the edges of the pan.
4 While the cream is heating, heat the golden syrup and sugar in another heavy pan until it reaches the hard-crack stage (154°C/310°F).

5 Add the butter and salt, then strain the cream mixture into the sugar mixture. Stir briefly to just combine, then bring the whole mixture back up to the firm-ball stage (120°C/248°F).
6 Stir in the toasted, chopped pecans. Retrieve and discard the vanilla pod.
7 Immediately pour into the foil cases, then lift the baking tray up and tamp it down to release any air bubbles. Top with gold leaf, if you like. Leave to cool completely.
8 Store the caramels in an airtight container at room temperature. They will keep for about 10 days.

Caramel apples

These delicious treats are popular at fairs and fêtes around the world. The buttery, chewy caramel contrasts wonderfully with the crisp apple, although eating these is a messy experience!

1 Wash and dry the apples. Push lollipop sticks or wooden dowels into the stem-end of the apples.

2 Prepare an ice-water bath and line a shallow baking tray with baking parchment.

3 Place all of the remaining ingredients in a large, heavy pan and heat gently over a medium heat. Stir to dissolve everything together into an emulsified mass.

4 Once the sugar has completely dissolved, bring the mixture to the boil and cook until it reaches the soft-ball stage (114°C/238°F).

5 Remove the caramel from the heat and arrest the cooking by placing the pan over the ice-water bath.

6 Leave the mixture to cool to 82°C/180°F before dipping the apples into the caramel, holding them by their sticks.

7 Place the caramel-covered apples on the parchment-lined baking sheet, stick- or dowel-end up, and allow them to cool.

8 If the caramel slips off the apple at all, leave it to cool slightly and dip again. Eat immediately or store in an airtight container at room temperature for 3 days.

makes: 8 caramel apples

8 small or medium eating apples

115g/4oz/½ cup unsalted butter

200g/7oz/1 cup granulated (white) sugar

150ml/¼ pint/⅔ cup double (heavy) cream

15ml/1 tbsp soft light brown sugar

125g/4¼oz golden (light corn) syrup

2.5ml/½ tsp vanilla extract

1.5ml/¼ tsp salt

Cook's Tip

Buy wooden dowels at a hardware or paint store. Use pruning shears to trim the dowels to the desired length. Dowels come in a few different widths. Choose ones that will be sturdy enough to hold on to while eating your apple.

Butterscotch

Depending on who you talk to, you will get a very different opinion on what is the most traditional of all sweets, but butterscotch will certainly be a popular choice. The butterscotch in this recipe is similar to a caramel, but the syrup is cooked a little longer to get a more brittle candy to suck on rather than chew.

makes: about 800g/1¾lb

400g/14oz/2 cups caster (superfine) or granulated (white) sugar

150ml/¼ pint/⅔ cup double (heavy) cream

150ml/¼ pint/⅔ cup water

1 vanilla pod (bean), split

1.5ml/¼ tsp cream of tartar

100g/3¾oz unsalted butter, cut into small cubes, plus extra for greasing

1 Grease a 20cm/8in square cake tin (pan), then line it with baking parchment so that the paper comes all the way up the sides.

2 Place the sugar, cream and water in a heavy pan over a low heat and stir gently until the sugar is dissolved.

3 Scrape the vanilla seeds from the pod into the pan and add the pod as well. Add the cream of tartar. Place over a medium heat and boil until the mixture reaches the soft-ball stage (114°C/238°F).

4 Add the butter and boil until the mixture reaches the soft-crack stage (143°C/290°F).

5 Pour the mixture into the prepared tin, retrieving and discarding the vanilla pod.

6 Let it cool slightly, then score the top to make it easier to break into squares when it is completely cooled.

7 When it is cold, break it into squares and wrap each piece in cellophane, waxed paper or foils. Store in an airtight container at room temperature. They will keep for about 10 days.

VARIATION: For chocolate butterscotch, add 15ml/1 tbsp cocoa powder to the pan with the sugar, cream and water.

Honey-sesame crunch

These are wholesome and energizing little confections. You often see a similar product in health food stores, but this version tastes much better. Densely packed with sesame seeds and lightly sweetened with honey and brown sugar, they make a great afternoon pick-me-up.

makes: about 400g/14oz

butter and grapeseed or groundnut (peanut) oil, for greasing

100g/3¾oz/8 tbsp soft light brown sugar

100g/3¾oz honey

200g/7oz raw sesame seeds

Cook's Tip
Health food stores are often the cheapest place to buy seeds.

1 Grease a baking sheet with butter and set aside. Grease a rolling pin with oil.
2 Combine the sugar and honey in a small, heavy pan and place over a low heat, stirring constantly, to emulsify.
3 Add the raw sesame seeds and stir for about 10 minutes until the seeds are golden-brown.
4 Pour the mixture out on to the prepared baking sheet and run the oiled rolling pin over it to smooth the surface and attain a thickness of about 5mm/¼in.

5 Leave to cool slightly, but cut it in to pieces while it is still warm or it will be too brittle and may shatter. Once cooled, keep in an airtight container or wrap each piece individually.

VARIATIONS: Try mixing different seeds into the mixture. Flax seeds are a good source of omega oils and taste delicious.
For a sweet and tangy version, add 25g/1oz finely chopped dried apricots with the sesame seeds.

Peanut brittle

The addition of bicarbonate of soda is what gives peanut brittle its unique texture. The raising action introduces thousands of tiny air bubbles into the sugar syrup, making it crunchy and airy. The stretching process also adds air and gives the brittle an almost opalescent quality.

1 Line a baking sheet with baking parchment and grease it lightly with oil.
2 Combine the sugar, golden syrup, salt and 60ml/4 tbsp water in a large, heavy pan. Heat gently over a low heat until the sugar dissolves.
3 Turn the heat up to medium and boil until the syrup reaches the hard-ball stage (130°C/266°F).
4 Add the peanuts and stir until the syrup reaches the hard-crack stage (154°C/310°F).

5 Remove the pan from the heat and stir in the butter and vanilla.
6 Dissolve the bicarbonate of soda in 5ml/1 tsp water and fold into the peanut mixture. Pour out on to the baking sheet.
7 Leave the mixture to cool until you can touch it. With oiled hands, pull the brittle from the sides, stretching it to make holes.
8 Leave to cool completely before breaking it up with the back of a spoon.
9 Serve immediately or store in an airtight container for a few days.

makes: about 600g/1lb 6oz

grapeseed or groundnut (peanut) oil, for greasing

175g/6oz/¾ cup caster (superfine) sugar

115g/4oz golden (light corn) syrup

5ml/1 tsp salt

250g/9oz raw peanuts

25g/1oz/2 tbsp unsalted butter, cubed

2.5ml/½ tsp vanilla extract

2.5ml/½ tsp bicarbonate of soda (baking soda)

Hazelnut praline

Hazelnuts are the nut of choice in this delectable crunchy treat. They need to be toasted to perfection – if under-toasted, the oils will not be released and if over-toasted, they will impart a bitter taste. This praline can be processed to a fine powder and sprinkled over ice cream or puddings.

1 Heat the oven to 180°C/350°F/Gas 4.
2 Spread the hazelnuts out on a baking sheet in one layer. Place in the oven. Set a timer for 7 minutes and then check them. They should have a golden colour and a good firm texture. Cook them for a little longer if necessary, checking them often, until they reach this stage.
3 Empty the tray into a clean dish towel and, while the nuts are still warm, rub the skins off with the towel.
4 Grease a sheet of baking parchment with butter and place it inside a baking tray. Transfer the toasted, skinned nuts on to it so they are in a single layer.

5 Now make the caramel. Combine the water, sugar and cream of tartar in a heavy pan. Place over a medium heat and bring to the boil, stirring to dissolve the sugar.
6 Once the sugar has dissolved stop stirring. Boil the syrup until it reaches the hard-crack stage (154°C/310°F), then continue cooking for 1 minute more.
7 Remove the pan from the heat and immediately pour the syrup over the toasted nuts.
8 Allow the caramel to cool completely before breaking it into bitesize pieces with your hands. Serve immediately or store in an airtight container.

makes: about 600g/1lb 6oz

200g/7oz whole hazelnuts, with skins

butter, for greasing

60ml/4 tbsp water

400g/14oz/2 cups caster (superfine) sugar

1.5ml/¼ tsp cream of tartar

Cook's Tip

Always buy the freshest nuts you can and use them quickly. Store nuts in airtight containers in the refrigerator or freezer. When buying hazelnuts, it is best to buy them with the skins on because the skinned ones have been blanched, further removing freshness and flavour. It is easy enough to skin them yourself.

Caramel-buttered popcorn

Gooey, buttery caramel-coated popcorn is a fabulous treat. This recipe is very simple and great to make with kids. They love the popping of the popcorn and will be especially delighted that they can eat the delicious results immediately.

makes: 300g/11oz

30ml/2 tbsp vegetable oil

100g/3¾oz dried popcorn kernels

100g/3¾oz salted butter

100g/3¾oz golden (light corn) syrup

1 Warm the oil in a heavy pan with a lid over a medium-high heat. Add the popcorn kernels and cover with the lid.
2 Cook, shaking occasionally, until the popping stops (after a few minutes). Remove the pan from the heat and open the lid to release a little steam. Set aside.

3 Melt the butter and golden syrup together in a separate large pan, stirring constantly to combine.
4 Transfer the popcorn into a large mixing bowl and pour over the syrup. Mix well. Serve immediately or keep for a few days in an airtight container or sealed bags.

Cook's Tip
A heavy-bottomed pan with a tight fitting lid will make this recipe much easier to achieve.

Peanut popcorn

makes: about 675g/1½lb

30ml/2 tbsp vegetable oil

100g/3¾oz dried popcorn kernels

25g/1oz salted butter

2.5ml/½ tsp salt

250g/9oz raw peanuts

225g/8oz golden (light corn) syrup

90g/3½oz soft dark brown sugar

2.5ml/½ tsp white wine or cider vinegar

Caramel coated peanuts and popcorn are a popular snack in the US, traditionally being sold in cardboard boxes. Today they are more likely to be sold in a bag, but the delicious flavours, replicated in this recipe, remain.

1 Warm the oil in a heavy pan with a lid over a medium-high heat. Add the popcorn and cover with the lid.

2 Cook, shaking occasionally, until the popping stops (after a few minutes). Turn off the heat and empty the popcorn into a large bowl.

3 Put the butter into the hot pan to melt it, then drizzle this over the popcorn. Sprinkle with the salt and toss. Stir in the peanuts.

4 Combine the golden syrup, brown sugar and vinegar in a separate heavy pan. Stir gently over a low heat to dissolve the sugar, then turn up the heat. Boil until it reaches the thread stage (111°C/233°F).

5 Pour the syrup over the popcorn and mix well. Spread out on to a baking sheet lined with baking parchment and leave it to cool completely before breaking apart. Serve immediately or keep for a few days in an airtight container or sealed bags.

FUDGES AND FRUIT AND NUT CONFECTIONS

There is an almost limitless range of recipes for fudges, but the success of all of them relies on exact proportions of ingredients, cooked to the correct temperature and combined with complementary flavours. Slightly less rich but just as delicious, confections made with fruit and nuts range from dense fruitcake to light, sweet coconut ice. They make a tasty treat at any time of the day.

Rich, creamy and coconutty

This chapter is filled with a wide range of intensely flavoured treats that are often best savoured in small amounts with friends and family on special occasions. They also make perfect gifts and are fun to experiment with.

Probably the most common home-made sweet is fudge, and it evokes comforting nostalgic images of grandmothers and children cooking together. Fudges are similar to toffees and caramels in that they are made up of exacting measures of sugar, water, cream, and butter. Its texture can vary, and there are countless flavour combinations. During cooking, the base mixture is taken to the soft-ball stage, when chocolate, vanilla, coffee, nut butters or a range of other flavours can be added. For textural interest, chopped nuts or candied peel can also be folded in. Some recipes call for beating the fudge while it is hot to make it grainy in texture. For the smoothest fudge, no stirring is recommended.

The famous Scottish sweet, tablet, is from the same family as fudge, although it is more firm and usually made with sweetened condensed milk rather than cream. It also makes a wonderful base for other flavours, such as vanilla or chopped fruits such as figs.

Italy is the home of the addictively spicy and fudgey fruitcake, Panforte. With its origins in 13th-century Siena, it is becoming increasingly popular on tables as far away from Italy as California and is a fabulous alternative to Christmas cake.

Coconuts and dates serve as a superb base for other confections such as Coconut Date Rolls or the old-time favourite, Coconut Ice. Both fruits can be used fresh or dry in sweet-making. Desiccated coconut is thoroughly dried to remove almost all of its moisture. Some dried coconut is then sweetened, which gives it the effect of being more moist. Fresh coconut is a wonderful ingredient and once you get over the anxiety of how to crack open the nut, it is actually quite easy to use. For best results, it is worth buying good-quality dried coconut and the right type of dates, and ensuring they are fresh.

Vanilla fudge

This classic recipe makes a delicious and simple fudge, which can be used as the base for a variety of different flavours. The beating of the mixture gives it the grainy texture that is typical of many fudges. If you like the grains to be larger, stir the fudge when it is hotter.

makes: about 1kg/2¼lb

300ml/½ pint/1¼ cups full-fat (whole) milk

½ vanilla pod (bean), seeds scraped

900g/2lb/4½ cups caster (superfine) sugar

125g/4¼ oz unsalted butter, cut into 1cm/½in cubes, plus extra for greasing

10ml/2 tsp vanilla extract

tiny pinch of salt

1 Grease a 20cm/8in square baking tin (pan) and line with baking parchment or waxed paper. Prepare an ice-water bath.

2 Put the milk, scraped vanilla seeds and pod, sugar and butter in a large, heavy pan and cook over a moderate heat, stirring constantly, until the sugar dissolves.

3 When the sugar is dissolved and the butter is melted, bring the mixture to the boil. Cover with a tight-fitting lid and cook for 2 minutes, then remove the lid.

4 Without stirring, let the mixture cook at a slow rolling boil for about 10 minutes, or until it reaches the soft-ball stage (114°C/238°F).

5 Immediately place the pan over the ice-water bath for a few seconds. Remove the vanilla pod with a fork or slotted spoon and discard. Stir in the vanilla extract and salt.

6 Place the pan in a cool part of the kitchen until it is lukewarm or about 43°C/110°F. Do not stir.

7 Once it reaches this temperature, beat with a wooden spoon until it is thick, smooth and creamy.

8 Pour into the prepared tin and leave it to cool completely.

9 Cut it into squares in the tin, then lift it out by the sides of the parchment and serve. Store in an airtight container.

Cook's Tip
Work quickly so the fudge doesn't have time to seize up.

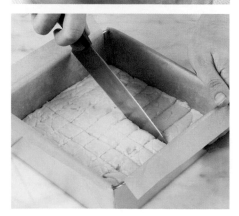

makes: about 1.2kg/2½lb

800g/1¾lb/4 cups caster (superfine) sugar

250ml/8fl oz/1 cup full-fat (whole) milk

75g/3oz/6 tbsp unsalted butter, cut into 1cm/½in cubes, plus extra for greasing

350g/12oz dark (bittersweet) chocolate (55–60% cocoa solids), cut into small pieces

5ml/1 tsp vanilla extract

Old-fashioned chocolate fudge

This timeless classic is a smooth fudge that is not worked, but instead is simply melted to the perfect temperature and poured into a tin to set. This version uses dark, intense chocolate, which cuts through the sweetness, but you could use milk chocolate if you prefer.

1 Grease a 20 x 30cm/8 x 12in rectangular baking tin (pan) and line with baking parchment or waxed paper. Prepare an ice-water bath.

2 Put the sugar, milk and butter in a large heavy pan and cook over a moderate heat, stirring constantly, until the sugar dissolves.

3 When the sugar is dissolved and the butter is melted, stop stirring. Bring the mixture to the boil.

4 Without stirring, let the mixture cook at a slow rolling boil for about 10 minutes, or until it reaches the soft-ball stage (114°C/238°F). Stir in the chocolate.

5 Immediately place the pan over the ice water bath for a few seconds. Stir in the vanilla extract. Pour into the tin. Leave to cool.

6 Lift out of the tin by the sides of the parchment paper and place on a chopping board. Cut into squares and serve. Store in an airtight container.

Almond milk fudge

This fudge is inspired by the popular Indian sweets made using almonds and clarified butter, and decorated with real silver leaf. The clarified butter gives it a nutty flavour, and the ground almonds give it a grainy texture.

makes: about 800g/1¾lb

115g/4oz/½ cup unsalted butter, plus extra for greasing

500ml/1¼lb double (heavy) cream

175g/6oz caster (superfine) sugar

500g/1¼lb ground almonds

edible silver or gold leaf (optional)

Cook's Tip
You could add a little orange blossom water or rose water to this fudge to make it more flavourful, but the simplicity of almonds, cream, sugar and butter is lovely.

1 Begin by clarifying the butter. Place the butter in a small pan on the lowest heat. Leave to melt without disturbing it.

2 When the butter has melted, skim any white foam off the top. The milk solids should have sunk to the bottom at this point, so pour the yellow, 'clarified' liquid into a jar, leaving any white milk solids behind. Don't worry about leaving a tiny amount of the fat in the pan if it means keeping the clarified butter completely free from the milk solids. Whatever you don't use can be kept in an airtight container in the refrigerator for up to two weeks.

3 Grease a 20cm/8in square baking tin (pan) and line with baking parchment.

4 Place the cream into a heavy pan over a moderate heat and bring to the boil.

5 Boil for about 10 minutes. Add the sugar and stir until dissolved.

6 Add the ground almonds and 50g/2oz of the clarified butter. Stir constantly for another five minutes, taking care not to let it scorch.

7 Pour the mixture into the prepared tin and press down with an offset spatula. Cover with a sheet of baking parchment and weight it down with a block of wood (such as a chopping board) and some weights. Allow it to cool for 10 minutes.

8 Remove the board and cover the surface with sheets of silver or gold leaf, if you like.

9 While the fudge is still slightly warm, cut it into diamond shapes. Allow it cool completely, then remove it from the tin and serve. Store in an airtight container.

Espresso-macadamia fudge

Macadamia nuts make the perfect partner for fudge, as their oily yet slightly crunchy texture complements the creamy texture of the fudge. The addition of coffee extract is merely to give it a little lift. If you own an espresso maker then by all means add a short shot of espresso in place of the coffee extract. A really strong blend would be absolutely delicious here. Be sure to use the freshest nuts possible, as macadamia nuts have a short shelf-life.

1 Grease a 20 x 30cm/8 x 12in rectangular baking tin (pan) and line with baking parchment or waxed paper.

2 Put the sugar, golden syrup and cream in a large, heavy pan and cook over a moderate heat, stirring constantly, until the sugar dissolves.

3 When the sugar has dissolved, bring the mixture to the boil.

4 Without stirring, let the mixture cook at a slow rolling boil for about 10 minutes, or until it reaches the soft-ball stage (114°C/238°F).

5 Remove the pan from the heat and quickly stir in the chocolate, nuts, butter, and coffee extract or espresso. Keep stirring until the chocolate and butter have melted and are thoroughly combined.

6 Pour the fudge mixture into the prepared baking tin and leave it to cool completely. This can take up to 8 hours.

7 Lift the fudge out of the tin by the sides of the parchment paper and place on a cutting surface.

8 Cut into squares and serve. Store in an airtight container.

makes: about 1.3kg/3lb

750g/1lb 11oz /3¾ cups caster (superfine) sugar

250ml/8fl oz/generous 1 cup golden (light corn) syrup

300ml/½ pint/1¼ cups double (heavy) cream

375g/13oz milk chocolate, chopped

250g/9oz macadamia nuts, chopped

75g/3oz/6 tbsp unsalted butter, cut into 1cm/½in cubes, plus extra for greasing

5ml/1 tsp coffee extract or instant espresso powder dissolved in 10ml/2 tsp boiling water

Candied clementine fudge

Divine nuggets of beautiful candied clementine peel make this fudge truly special. You should definitely try making your own candied peel, as the flavour will be much brighter and truer. In order to buy it, you will need to go to speciality delis or department stores with food halls. If all else fails, you can make this fudge with candied orange or lemon peel instead.

1 Grease a 20 x 30cm/8 x 12in rectangular baking tin (pan) and line with baking parchment or waxed paper.

2 Put the sugar, golden syrup, cream, butter and clementine zest in a large, heavy pan and cook over moderate heat, stirring constantly, until the sugar dissolves.

3 When the sugar has dissolved and the butter has melted, bring it to the boil.

4 Without stirring, let the mixture cook at a slow rolling boil for about 10 minutes, or until it reaches the soft-ball stage (114°C/238°F).

5 Remove the pan from the heat and stir in the white chocolate, 100g/3¾oz of the candied peel, the clementine juice and lemon juice.

6 Pour the mixture into the baking tin and scatter over the remaining chopped peel.

7 Leave it to cool completely. This can take up to 8 hours.

8 Lift the fudge out of the tin by the sides of the parchment paper and place on a cutting surface.

9 Cut into squares and serve. Store in an airtight container.

makes: about 1.3kg/3lb

750g/1lb 11oz /3¾ cups caster (superfine) sugar

50ml/2fl oz/¼ cup golden (light corn) syrup

300ml/½ pint/1¼ cups double (heavy) cream

100g/3¾oz unsalted butter, cut into 1cm/½in cubes

15ml/1 tbsp clementine zest

350g/12oz white chocolate, chopped

150g/5oz candied clementine peel, chopped

30ml/2 tbsp clementine juice

30ml/2 tbsp lemon juice

750g/1lb 11oz caster (superfine) sugar

250ml/8fl oz/generous 1 cup golden
(light corn) syrup

300ml/½ pint/1¼ cups double
(heavy) cream

75g/3oz/6 tbsp unsalted butter, cut into
1cm/½ in cubes

200g/7oz smooth, natural peanut butter

150g/5oz roasted and salted
peanuts, chopped

100g/3¾oz milk chocolate
(64% cocoa solids), chopped

Peanut butter fudge

This fudge has a fabulous texture. The combination of smooth, creamy peanut butter and melted milk chocolate result in a silkiness that cannot be attained any other way. Use a high-quality natural peanut butter with no added sugars or fats.

1 Grease a 20cm/8in square baking tin (pan) and line with baking parchment or waxed paper.

2 Put the sugar, golden syrup, cream and butter in a large, heavy pan and cook over a moderate heat, stirring constantly, until the sugar dissolves.

3 When the sugar has dissolved and the butter has melted, bring the mixture to the boil.

4 Without stirring, let the mixture cook at a slow rolling boil for about 10 minutes, or until it reaches the soft-ball stage (114°C/238°F).

5 Remove from the heat and stir in the peanut butter. Gently fold in the nuts and chopped chocolate.

6 Pour into the prepared baking tin and leave it to cool completely. This can take up to 8 hours.

7 Lift the fudge out of the tin by the sides of the parchment paper and place on a cutting surface. Cut into squares and serve. Store in an airtight container.

VARIATION: You could also use crunchy peanut butter if you prefer, but it will change the consistency of the fudge.

Yogurt pecan fudge

This delectable treat is similar to penuche fudge, in which brown sugar is the main flavouring. In this modern twist, yogurt is used in place of double cream for a lighter, tangier flavour.

1 Combine the yogurt and bicarbonate of soda in a large, heavy pan and set aside for 20 minutes.

2 Grease a 20cm/8in round or square baking tin (pan) and line with baking parchment. Prepare an ice-water bath.

3 Add the sugar and golden syrup to the yogurt mixture and place the pan over a moderate heat, stirring to dissolve the sugar.

4 When the sugar has dissolved, bring the mixture to the boil, then add the butter. Boil until the syrup reaches the soft-ball stage (114°C/238°F).

5 Remove from the heat and immediately dip the base of the pan into the ice-water bath for a few seconds. Set aside and leave to cool until the mixture is lukewarm (about 50°C/122°F).

6 Beat until creamy, then add the chopped nuts. Pour into the prepared baking tin. Leave it to cool completely. This can take up to 8 hours.

7 Lift the fudge out of the tin by the sides of the baking parchment and place on a cutting surface. Cut into thin wedges and serve. Store in an airtight container.

makes: about 550g/1lb 4oz

225ml/7½fl oz/scant 1 cup natural (plain) yogurt

5ml/1 tsp bicarbonate of soda (baking soda)

400g/14oz/2 cups soft light brown sugar

30ml/2 tbsp golden (light corn) syrup

60g/2½oz unsalted butter, plus extra for greasing

150g/5oz chopped, toasted pecans

Cook's Tip
Do not use Greek (US strained plain) yogurt in this recipe.

Rocky road fudge

Most often associated with ice cream, rocky road is a classic US treat. A cool way to present this is to put it into a loaf tin and then slice it like a terrine when it is set. Be warned, this is very rich, so a thin slice will suffice!

1 Line a loaf tin (pan) (about 10 x 23cm/ 4 x 9in) with clear film (plastic wrap) so that it comes out of the tin and well over the sides.

2 Put the sugar, milk and butter in a medium, heavy pan. Heat over a moderate heat, stirring constantly, until the sugar has dissolved.

3 Chop the walnuts roughly and set aside.

4 When the sugar has dissolved and the butter has melted, bring the mixture to the boil. Without stirring, allow the mixture to cook at a slow rolling boil for about 10 minutes, or until it reaches the soft-ball stage (114°C/238°F).

5 Stir in the chopped chocolate, vanilla extract and salt.

6 Pour about one-third of the chocolate fudge mixture into the prepared baking tin. Sprinkle with half of the cherries, marshmallows and walnuts. Cover with another third of the chocolate fudge. Sprinkle with the remaining cherries, marshmallows and walnuts. Cover with the remaining third of chocolate fudge.

7 Place a piece of baking parchment over the fudge and press it down firmly with your hands. Set aside to cool. This could take up to 8 hours.

8 When ready to serve, lift the fudge up out of the tin by holding the sides of the clear film and transfer to a chopping board. Cut 1cm/½in slices and serve. Store in an airtight container for up to 1 week.

makes: about 3kg/6¾lb

1.4kg/3lb 2oz/7 cups castor (superfine) sugar

500ml/17fl oz/generous 2 cups full-fat (whole) milk

150g/5oz/10 tbsp unsalted butter, cut into 1cm/½in cubes

75g/3oz walnuts

700g/1lb 11oz dark (bittersweet) chocolate (55–60% cocoa solids), cut into small pieces

10ml/2 tsp vanilla extract

1.5ml/¼ tsp salt

90g/3½oz amarena cherries or sour cherries in syrup, sliced in half

130g/4½oz marshmallows, cut into pieces, or use mini marshmallows

Vanilla tablet

Scotch tablet is a hybrid of fudge and toffee that dates back to the 18th century in Scotland. It has a grainy texture, similar to fudge, but is harder. Traditionally it was made using just sugar and cream, but since this has a tendency to burn, the recipe has been adapted to incorporate sweetened condensed milk.

makes: about 1kg/2¼lb

900g/2lb/4½ cups caster (superfine) sugar

125g/4¼oz unsalted butter, plus extra for greasing

150ml/¼ pint/⅔ cup water

150ml/¼ pint/⅔ cup full-fat (whole) milk

1 vanilla pod (bean)

200ml/7fl oz/scant 1 cup sweetened condensed milk

1 Grease a 20cm/8in square baking tin (pan) or 23cm/9in square baking dish. Line with baking parchment. Set aside.

2 Put the sugar, butter, water and milk in a large, heavy pan and stir over a low heat to combine.

3 Split the vanilla bean down the centre and scrape the seeds from inside with a small knife. Add them and the scraped pod to the pan.

4 Stir gently until the sugar has dissolved, then turn the heat up to medium and bring to the boil. Do not stir the syrup at this point as this could cause crystallization.

5 Boil the mixture until it reaches the soft-ball stage (114°C/238°F), then stir in the condensed milk. Bring back up to 116°C/240°F, then remove from the heat.

6 Leave to cool for 5 minutes. Remove the vanilla pod with a fork and discard.

7 Stir the syrup vigorously with a wooden spoon until it becomes creamy and lighter in colour. This may take a few minutes.

8 Pour through a sieve (strainer) into the tin. Leave to set and cool for a few hours.

9 Turn out on to a chopping board and cut it into squares to serve. Store in an airtight container.

Cook's Tip
When you remove the vanilla pod, instead of discarding it, you can rinse it and dry it out near an open oven. Place it in a jar of sugar and leave for a few days to create vanilla-flavoured sugar.

Fig tablet

This recipe has a wonderful texture: fudgy tablet bursting with fig seeds. Tablet is delicious combined with any dried fruits, such as apricots or prunes. Don't use fresh figs as they hold too much juice and the tablet won't set properly.

1 Grease a 20cm/8in square baking tin (pan) or 23cm/9in square baking dish and line with baking parchment. Set aside.
2 Place the chopped figs in a small bowl and cover with boiling water. Set aside to soak for about 30 minutes.
3 Put the milk, water, butter, salt and sugar in a heavy pan and stir over a low heat to combine.
4 Split the vanilla bean down the centre and scrape the seeds from inside with a small knife. Add them and the scraped pod to the pan.
5 Stir gently until the sugar is dissolved, then turn the heat up to medium and bring to the boil.
6 Boil the mixture until it reaches the soft-ball stage (114°C/238°F).
7 Meanwhile, strain the figs and pat dry with kitchen paper.

8 When the syrup has reached the correct temperature, stir in the figs.
9 Remove from the heat and leave to cool for 5 minutes. Remove the vanilla pod with a fork and discard.
10 Stir the syrup vigorously with a wooden spoon until it becomes creamy and lighter in colour. This may take a few minutes.
11 Pour into the prepared tin and leave it to set and cool.
12 Turn out on to a chopping board and cut it into squares to serve. Store in an airtight container.

VARIATIONS: Substitute the figs with desiccated (dry unsweetened) coconut and add 15ml/1 tbsp Bacardi rum or Malibu.

It is perfectly fine to use 10ml/2 tbsp vanilla extract in place of the vanilla pod for a more economical version of the recipe.

makes: about 1.3kg/3lb

100g/3¾oz dried figs, chopped

150ml/¼ pint/⅔ cup full-fat (whole) milk

150ml/¼ pint/⅔ cup water

50g/2oz unsalted butter, plus extra for greasing

2.5ml/½ tsp salt

900g/2lb caster (superfine) or granulated (white) sugar

1 vanilla pod (bean)

Sour cherry panforte

Panforte is a dense, spicy Italian fruitcake, made by stirring a range of ingredients into a fudgey sugar syrup. The cake is said to contain 17 ingredients to represent the 17 municipal wards, or 'contrade', of Siena – the town that is famous for this speciality. There are records of panforte going as far back as the 13th century.

1 Preheat the oven to 170°C/340°F/ Gas 3½. Spread the whole almonds out on a baking sheet lined with baking parchment and place in the oven for about 12 minutes. Test to see if they are done by tasting one. They should just be starting to look golden inside and taste lightly toasted.

2 Transfer the almonds to a large mixing bowl and set aside. Reduce the oven temperature to 150°C/300°F/Gas 2.

3 Grease two 15–18cm/6–7in round cake tins (pans). Cut circles of rice paper to line the bottoms of the tins and then cut strips to line the sides.

4 Chop all of the candied peel and the dried cherries into small, even pieces. Add the fruit to the toasted nuts in the bowl.

5 Sift together the flour, salt, cinnamon, nutmeg, black pepper, cloves and cayenne and add to the fruit and nuts.

6 Combine the honey, sugar and golden syrup in a heavy pan. Heat until the mixture reaches the soft-ball stage (114°C/238°F).

7 Add all of the prepared ingredients in the bowl to the pan and stir quickly to combine. Transfer to the prepared tins.

8 Place the tins in the oven and bake for 35 minutes exactly.

9 Remove from the oven and leave to cool in the tins.

10 When cool, carefully turn out on to a serving dish. Sift over icing sugar, cut into wedges and serve immediately. Store in an airtight container for up to 2 weeks.

makes: 2 cakes

500g/1¼lb whole almonds, skins on

butter, for greasing

4 sheets of rice paper

100g/3¾oz candied citron peel

100g/3¾oz candied lemon peel

200g/7oz candied orange or clementine peel

200g/7oz dried sour cherries

250g/9oz/2½ cups plain (all-purpose) flour

2.5ml/½ tsp salt

5ml/1 tsp ground cinnamon

2.5ml/½ tsp freshly grated nutmeg

2.5ml/½ tsp ground black pepper

2.5ml/½ tsp ground cloves

0.75ml/⅛ tsp ground cayenne pepper

350g/12oz/scant 1 cup honey

300g/11oz/1½ cups granulated (white) sugar

175g/6oz/scant ½ cup golden (light corn) syrup

icing (confectioners') sugar, for dusting

makes: 36 coconut date rolls

36 good-quality dates, such as Medjool

150g/5oz desiccated
(dry unsweetened) coconut

Cook's Tip
These sweets make the perfect gift
and look very smart when presented
in a gift box tied with ribbon.

Coconut date rolls

Incredibly simple to make and attractive as after-dinner treats, these little
morsels were once found primarily in health food shops. High in fibre, they
are indeed better for you than many other confections, but they taste none
the worse for it! Use unsweetened coconut rather than the sweetened variety.

1 Cut the dates in half and remove the
stones (pits) with a small knife.
2 If you are using Medjool dates, which
tend to be firmer than other types, place
in a small pan with 15ml/1 tbsp water.
Simmer for 5 minutes, or until softened.
3 Push the dates through a sieve
(strainer) into a bowl positioned
underneath using the back of a spoon.

4 Roll the pulped dates into small oval
balls, about the same size and shape as
the dates were originally.
5 Put the coconut in a shallow bowl or
saucer and roll the date balls in it.
6 Place the coconut date rolls in
individual miniature paper cases and
serve immediately. Store in an airtight
container for a few days.

Coconut ice

The pink food colouring here is optional, but it looks lovely and similar to the iconic store-bought variety that is loved throughout the world. The use of coconut milk instead of milk in this version really enhances the coconut taste. You could also add a splash of rum, which helps to cut the sweetness.

makes: about 1.3kg/3lb

butter, for greasing

750g/1lb 13oz/3¾ cups caster (superfine) sugar

300ml/½ pint/1¼ cups coconut milk

2.5ml/½ tsp salt

275g/10oz desiccated (dry unsweetened) coconut

2–3 drops pink food colouring (optional), or any other colour you like

1 Grease a 20cm/8in square tin (pan) and line with baking parchment or waxed paper.
2 Combine the sugar, coconut milk and salt in a heavy pan and stir over a medium heat until the sugar has dissolved.
3 Bring the mixture to the boil, add the desiccated coconut and stir to combine.
4 Pour two-thirds of the mixture into the prepared tin. Combine the remaining one-third with a few drops of pink food colouring in the pan, then quickly pour over the first layer in the tin.

5 Smooth the top with an offset spatula, pressing down slightly.
6 Allow the coconut ice to cool completely. This may take a few hours.
7 Lift out of the tin by the sides of the parchment or waxed paper and place on a cutting surface. Cut into squares and serve. Store in an airtight container.

VARIATIONS: You could replace the coconut milk with an equal quantity of full-fat (whole) milk.

Chocolate macaroons

These macaroons combine moist coconut with dark chocolate, and are a popular variety of cookie in the US. In this recipe the cookies are chewy with a slightly toasted outer edge, filled with dark chocolate. Eat them before the chocolate has set completely to experience them at their best.

1 Preheat the oven to 160°C/325°F/ Gas 3. Line a baking sheet with baking parchment.

2 Combine all of the ingredients, except the chocolate, in a heavy pan and cook over a medium heat for about 7 minutes, stirring constantly, until the mixture is opaque and sticky. The coconut should just begin to scorch on the bottom of the pan.

3 Transfer the coconut mixture to a mixing bowl and allow it to cool completely.

4 Drop tablespoonfuls of the mixture on to the baking sheet.

5 Using the end of a wooden spoon, make small depressions in the centre of each macaroon.

6 Place in the oven and bake for about 12 minutes, until the macaroons are just golden around the edges.

7 Place the chocolate in a heatproof bowl and position over a pan of barely simmering water, making sure the water does not touch the bowl. Leave until the chocolate is melted.

8 Transfer the melted chocolate to a piping (pastry) bag with a fine nozzle and fill the indented centre of each macaroon with chocolate.

9 Leave to cool, until the chocolate is almost set, then serve immediately. These macaroons are best eaten on the day they are made, but they can be stored in an airtight container for up to 1 week.

makes: about 18 cookies

2 egg whites

125g/4¼oz caster (superfine) sugar

0.75ml/⅛ tsp salt

10ml/2 tsp honey

100g/3¾oz desiccated (dry unsweetened) coconut

0.5ml/½ tsp vanilla extract

100g/3¾oz dark (bittersweet) chocolate, broken into pieces

Cook's Tip
Instead of using a piping (pastry) bag, you could put the melted chocolate in a sealable food storage bag. Tip the bag so the chocolate is in one corner, then snip off the corner of the bag to make a small hole through which the chocolate can be piped.

MARSHMALLOWS, NOUGATS AND SUGAR SHAPES

Egg whites are the main ingredient in this collection of melt-in-your mouth recipes. From light-as-air marshmallows to dense and delectable nougats, these confections transform simple sugar syrup and fresh egg whites into pretty and tasty treats. For special occasions, it is well worth having a go at moulding sugar to make sugar mice or a sweet alternative to the traditional chocolate Easter egg.

Soft, squishy and sophisticated

Melt-in-the-mouth marshmallows are always a hit with kids, whether eaten as they are, toasted around a fire, coated in chocolate or served on top of a cup of frothy hot chocolate. They consist of a sugar syrup that has been cooked to the hard-ball stage before dissolved gelatine is added. This is then poured into whipped egg whites and beaten to a light and fluffy mixture that can be easily transferred into a prepared tin (pan) to set. If you are whipping egg whites in anything other than a copper bowl, it is always advisable to add a pinch of cream of tartar. This will stabilize the whites and allow you to create perfect peaks. Once the mixture is set, it can be turned out of the tin on to a dusted board and cut into individual portions with a knife or pastry (cookie) cutters.

Nougat has the same sugar syrup and egg white base, but it is pressed once it has been poured into the tin to remove most of the air. The resulting texture is gooey and sticky to the touch, but it disappears in your mouth. Honey is also a key ingredient in nougat, but it must be added after the syrup has cooked or the flavour will be altered. Almonds, pistachios and rose or orange blossom waters are common additions. Nougat is usually sandwiched between two layers of edible rice paper, which is very thin and tasteless, and sometimes pressed under weights overnight. It is then sliced into neat bars, revealing the gooey, sugary and nutty consistency – irresistible.

Divinity and meringues are dropped shapes made from a similar concoction of sugar syrup and egg whites. Divinity is set by taking sugar syrup to the firm-ball stage and adding it to whipped egg whites. Meringues are made by adding sugar to whipped egg whites, which is then set in the oven at a low temperature over a long period of time.

Sugar shapes are made by pressing sugar and egg whites or meringue powder (pasteurized egg whites in powdered form) into a mould and allowing it to set. Another way to make them is to shape pre-made fondant into the shapes you desire and then embellish them with decorations.

Vanilla bean marshmallows

makes: about 900g/2lb

vegetable oil, for greasing

50g/2oz/½ cup icing (confectioners') sugar

50g/2oz/½ cup cornflour (cornstarch)

2 egg whites

400g/14oz/2 cups caster (superfine) sugar

15ml/1 tbsp glucose syrup

½ vanilla pod (bean), split and seeds scraped

375ml/13fl oz cold water

60ml/4 tbsp powdered gelatine

20ml/2 tbsp vanilla extract

Fluffy and delicious, home-made marshmallows have a different texture to store-bought ones because they are meant to be eaten within days, not months, so are not full of preservatives. You can add many flavours and colours to them.

1 Grease a baking tray. Combine the icing sugar and cornflour in a large bowl. Pass the mixture through a sieve (strainer) into another bowl positioned underneath to ensure it is well mixed. Liberally sift some of the mixture over the greased baking tray.

2 Whisk the egg whites until they form firm peaks (preferably in a stand mixer or with a powerful hand-held electric whisk). Set aside. They will separate slightly, but you can whisk them up again quickly just before you need them.

3 Combine the caster sugar, glucose syrup, scraped vanilla pod and the seeds, and half of the water in a small pan over a low heat. Stir to dissolve the sugar.

4 Bring the syrup to a boil and boil until it reaches the hard-ball stage (130°C/266°F).

5 Meanwhile, soften the gelatine with the remaining cold water in a small pan, off the heat. Just before the sugar syrup reaches the hard-ball stage, place the gelatine mixture over a low heat and stir to dissolve.

6 When the syrup reaches the correct temperature and the gelatine has dissolved, combine the two. Stir in the vanilla extract.

7 Turn the electric whisk on again and whisk the egg whites constantly while pouring in the syrup and gelatine mixture in a slow, steady stream. Continue until all of the mixture has been incorporated.

8 Whisk the mixture on a medium-high heat for at least 7 minutes, until it is almost stiff. Pour into the prepared baking tray and smooth the top with an offset spatula. Allow to set for about 5 hours.

9 Dust a work surface with most of the cornflour and icing sugar mixture, and turn the marshmallows out on to it by carefully inverting the baking tray. Cut into cubes and allow to dry out for a couple of hours.

10 Serve, or store in an airtight container or in cellophane bags. Dust with the remaining cornflour-icing sugar mixture to prevent the marshmallows from sticking together.

VARIATION: To make peppermint marshmallows, omit the vanilla pod in step 3. Add 10ml/2 tsp peppermint extract and 2.5ml/½ tsp green food colouring to the dissolved gelatine at the end of step 5, before stirring it into the syrup. Continue as above.

Raspberry heart marshmallows

makes: about 800g/1¾lb

vegetable oil, for greasing

50g/2oz/½ cup icing (confectioners') sugar

50g/2oz/½ cup cornflour (cornstarch)

2 egg whites

400g/14oz/2 cups caster (superfine) sugar

15ml/1 tbsp glucose syrup

175ml/6fl oz/¾ cup cold water

60ml/4 tbsp powdered gelatine

200ml/7fl oz/scant 1 cup puréed raspberries (*see* Cook's Tip)

10ml/2 tsp vanilla extract

Cook's Tips

∗ To make the raspberry purée, place 350g/12oz raspberries in a small pan and cook for about 10 minutes until they release their juices. Strain through a sieve (strainer), using the back of a spoon to get all the juices.

∗ Cutting these lovely pink marshmallows into heart shapes makes them look really special, particularly for a romantic occasion such as Valentine's Day, when they look especially charming floating in a cup of hot chocolate.

You can add almost any flavour to marshmallows. Berry-flavoured ones are especially wonderful because of the acidity in the fruit, which balances well with the sweetness of the fluffy sugary mass. The colour of the berries also transfers to the finished sweets, in this case creating a delicate soft pink.

1 Grease a baking tray. Combine the icing sugar and cornflour in a large bowl. Pass the mixture through a sieve (strainer) into another bowl positioned underneath to ensure it is well mixed. Liberally sift some of the mixture over the oiled baking tray.

2 Whisk the egg whites until they form firm peaks (preferably in a stand mixer or with a powerful hand-held electric whisk). Set aside. They will separate slightly, but you can whisk them up again quickly just before you need them.

3 Combine the sugar, glucose syrup and 75ml/5 tbsp cold water in a small pan over low heat. Stir to dissolve the sugar.

4 Bring the syrup to a boil and boil until it reaches the hard-ball stage (130°C/266°F).

5 Meanwhile, soften the gelatine with the remaining cold water in a small pan, off the heat. Just before the sugar syrup reaches the hard-ball stage, place the gelatine mixture over a low heat and stir to dissolve.

6 When the syrup reaches the correct temperature and the gelatine has dissolved, combine the two and whisk by hand.

7 Add the raspberry purée and the vanilla extract and stir to combine.

8 Turn the electric whisk on again and whisk the egg whites constantly while pouring in the syrup and gelatine mixture in a slow, steady stream. Continue until all of the mixture has been incorporated.

9 Whisk the mixture on medium-high for at least 7 minutes, until it is almost stiff. Pour into the prepared baking tray and smooth the top with an offset spatula. Allow to set for about 5 hours.

10 Dust a work surface with most of the remaining cornflour and icing sugar mixture and turn the marshmallows out on to it by carefully inverting the baking tray.

11 Cut the mixture into heart-shapes with a shaped cookie cutter and allow to dry out for a couple of hours.

12 Serve immediately or store in an airtight container. Dust with the remaining cornflour-icing sugar mixture to prevent the marshmallows from sticking together. These make a wonderful gift, presented in a cellophane bag tied with a ribbon.

Two-tone marshmallow sticks

 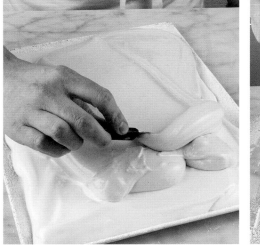 

makes: about 900g/2lb

vegetable oil, for greasing

50g/2oz/½ cup icing (confectioners') sugar

50g/2oz/½ cup cornflour (cornstarch)

2 egg whites

400g/14oz/2 cups caster (superfine) sugar

15ml/1 tbsp glucose syrup

375ml/13fl oz cold water

60ml/4 tbsp powdered gelatine

5ml/1 tsp vanilla extract

3 drops pink food colouring

3 drops yellow food colouring

This classic recipe for pretty two-tone marshmallows is a joy to make. The end result is wonderful in both colour and texture. Serve them as they are, or try twisting them or tying them into pretzel-like knots.

1 Grease a baking tray. Combine the icing sugar and cornflour in a large bowl. Pass the mixture through a sieve (strainer) into another bowl positioned underneath to ensure it is well mixed. Liberally sift some of the mixture over the oiled baking tray. Set aside.

2 Whisk the egg whites until they form firm peaks (preferably in a stand mixer or with a powerful hand-held electric whisk). Set aside. They will separate slightly, but you can whisk them up again quickly just before you need them.

3 Combine the caster sugar, glucose syrup, scraped vanilla pod and the seeds and half of the water in a small pan over a low heat. Stir to dissolve the sugar.

4 Bring the syrup to a boil and boil until it reaches the hard-ball stage (130°C/266°F).

5 Meanwhile, soften the gelatine with the remaining cold water in a small pan, off the heat. Just before the sugar syrup reaches the hard-ball stage, place the gelatine mixture over a low heat and stir to dissolve.

6 When the syrup reaches the correct temperature and the gelatine has dissolved, combine the two. Stir in the vanilla extract.

7 Turn the electric whisk on again and whisk the egg whites constantly while pouring in the syrup and gelatine mixture in a slow, steady stream. Continue until all of the mixture has been incorporated.

8 Whisk the mixture on medium-high for at least 7 minutes, until it holds soft peaks.

9 Divide the mixture between two bowls and add a different food colouring to each. Using an electric whisk or a stand mixer, whisk the mixture until almost stiff.

10 Pour the yellow marshmallow mixture into the prepared baking tray and spread it evenly.

11 Quickly spread the pink marshmallow on top of the yellow marshmallow. Allow to set for about 5 hours.

12 Dust the top with the remaining icing sugar and cornflour mixture, then cut the marshmallow into strips using an oiled knife.

13 Serve immediately or store in an airtight container. Dust the strips with extra cornflour and icing sugar mixture to keep the marshmallow strips from sticking together, if you are storing them.

Almond meringue kisses

These nutty kisses should be slightly gooey in the middle and simply melt in your mouth. The salt in this recipe really brings out the toasty almond flavour. To add an extra dimension you could dip them in melted chocolate.

makes: about 250g/9oz

100g/3¾oz flaked almonds

2 egg whites

115g/4oz/1 cup icing (confectioners') sugar

0.75ml/⅛ tsp salt

2.5ml/½ tsp vanilla extract

Cook's Tip
Always make sure your bowls and equipment are scrupulously clean with no trace of grease when whipping up egg whites. Adding a pinch of cream of tartar to the egg whites can help them whip up better.

1 Preheat the oven to 180°C/350°F and line two baking sheets with baking parchment or silicone mats.

2 Spread the almonds out on another baking sheet and toast for about seven minutes until golden brown. Leave to cool.

3 Smash up the cooled almonds with a rolling pin into pieces that will fit through a piping bag.

4 Combine the egg whites, icing sugar and salt in a stainless steel bowl. Place over a pan of just-simmering water. Whisk the ingredients to combine, then continue whisking until the whites reach 49°C/120°F.

5 Take the whites off the heat and transfer to a stand mixer or use a hand-held mixer with a whisk attachment. Add the vanilla extract.

6 Whip the whites until stiff, glossy peaks form. Lightly fold in the chopped toasted almonds.

7 Working quickly, scoop the contents into a piping (pastry) bag fitted with a large, round tip and pipe tablespoon-size blobs on to the prepared baking sheets, about 2.5cm/1in apart. Pull away from the tops quickly so little points form.

8 Place in the preheated oven and keep the door ajar with a wooden spoon. Cook for about 20 minutes, until you can move the meringues along the paper easily. If they stick to the paper, they need another 1–2 minutes. Bake for less time if you want the inside a little more gooey.

9 Serve the kisses immediately, or store in an airtight container.

Strawberry meringue clouds

These little sandwiches of meringue and strawberry-flavoured cream are even more delicious if they are assembled an hour or so before serving and placed in an airtight container in the refrigerator to chill them through.

1 Preheat the oven to 180°C/350°F. Line two baking sheets with baking parchment or silicone mats.

2 Combine the egg whites, icing sugar and salt in a stainless steel bowl. Place over a pan of just-simmering water. Whisk the ingredients to combine, then continue whisking until the whites reach 49°C/120°F.

3 Transfer to a stand mixer or use a hand-held mixer with a whisk attachment. Add the vanilla extract and whip the whites until stiff, glossy peaks form.

4 Working quickly, scoop the contents into a piping (pastry) bag fitted with a large, round tip and pipe tablespoon-size blobs on to the prepared baking sheets, about 2.5cm/1in apart. Pull away from the tops quickly so little points form.

5 Place in the oven and keep the door ajar with a wooden spoon. Cook for about 20 minutes, until you can move them along the paper easily. If they stick to the paper, they need another 1–2 minutes.

6 Leave the meringues to cool completely, then pull them up from the paper, resting them back down on their sides.

7 Whip the double cream into soft peaks. Add the sugar to the strawberry and raspberry purées, then fold into the cream.

8 Fill a piping bag with the cream and pipe a blob on to the flat underside of half of the cooled meringues. Taking the remaining meringues, make little sandwiches and place them in paper cups or pile high on a serving plate. Chill for an hour or, if you prefer, serve immediately.

makes: about 600g/1lb 6oz

2 egg whites

115g/4oz/1 cup icing (confectioners') sugar

0.75ml/⅛ tsp salt

2.5ml/½ tsp vanilla extract

300ml/½ pint/1¼ cups double (heavy) cream

100g/3¾oz strawberry purée (see Cook's Tip on page 82 – use 200g/8oz strawberries)

50g/2oz raspberry purée (see Cook's Tip on page 82 – use 100g/4oz raspberries)

30ml/2 tbsp caster (superfine) sugar

Melting chocolate meringues

These little meringues are both chewy and crunchy, and filled with delectable flecks of chocolate. When they are baked perfectly, the meringue is slightly gooey and, if they are fresh from the oven, the chocolate is slightly melted.

1 Preheat the oven to 180°C/350°F. Line two baking sheets with baking parchment or silicone mats.
2 Combine the egg whites, icing sugar and salt in a stainless steel bowl. Place over a pan of just-simmering water. Whisk the ingredients to combine, then continue whisking until the whites reach 49°C/120°F.
3 Take the whites off the heat and transfer to a stand mixer or use a hand-held mixer with a whisk attachment. Add the vanilla extract and whip the whites until stiff and glossy peaks form. Fold in the chocolate.

4 Scoop the contents into a piping (pastry) bag fitted with a large, round tip and pipe tablespoon-size blobs on to the baking sheets, about 2.5cm/1in apart. Pull away from the tops quickly so little points form.
5 Place into the oven and keep the door ajar with a wooden spoon. Cook for about 20 minutes, until you can move them along the paper easily. If they stick to the paper, they need 1–2 minutes more. Bake for less time if you want the inside more gooey.
6 Leave to cool completely. Serve immediately or store in airtight container.

makes: about 250g/9oz

2 egg whites

115g/4oz/1 cup icing (confectioners') sugar

0.75ml/⅛ tsp salt

2.5ml/½ tsp vanilla extract

100g/3¾oz dark (bittersweet) chocolate, chopped into pea-size chunks

Sea foam

This delicious sweet is so named because of its resemblance to the sea foam that forms along the coast of the Irish Sea, where the sweet was originally made. Made with soft light brown sugar, it is a soft caramel colour studded with nuggets of crystallized ginger, which cuts the sweetness and gives it a spicy bite.

makes: about 500g/1¼lb

160g/5¼oz soft light brown sugar

160g/5¼oz granulated (white) or caster (superfine) sugar

15ml/1 tbsp glucose syrup

0.75ml/⅛ tsp salt

50ml/2fl oz/¼ cup water

1 egg white

125g/4¼oz crystallized ginger, chopped into 5mm/¼in dice

1 Line a baking sheet with baking parchment or waxed paper.

2 Put the sugars, glucose syrup, salt and water in a heavy pan. Place over a medium heat.

3 Stir to dissolve the sugar, then raise the heat. Boil the syrup until it reaches the firm-ball stage (120°C/248°F).

4 Meanwhile, whisk the egg white in a clean bowl until if forms firm peaks.

5 When the syrup is ready, pour it into the egg white, whisking the whole time.

6 Whip up into almost-firm peaks, then add the chopped crystallized ginger and stir to combine.

7 Drop spoonfuls of the mixture on to the baking parchment or waxed paper. They should be irregular in shape, like sea foam scooped from the seashore.

8 Leave to set up for about 20 minutes before serving. Transfer to mini paper cases if they are for a special occasion.

9 Store in an airtight container for up to 1 week.

Walnut and apricot divinity

makes: about 575g/1lb 7oz

75g/3oz dried apricots

75g/3oz walnuts

325g/11½oz granulated (white) or caster (superfine) sugar

50ml/2fl oz/¼ cup glucose syrup or golden (light corn) syrup

0.75ml/⅛ tsp salt

50ml/2fl oz/¼ cup water

1 egg white

5ml/1 tsp vanilla extract

In the southern states of the US, divinity is a very common sweet. It is often made with pecans, but the soft texture of fresh walnuts is delicious with this meringue-like treat. The addition of chopped dried apricots adds a contrast in flavour and a little colour, making these a decadent autumnal treat.

1 Line a baking sheet with baking parchment or waxed paper.

2 Chop the apricots and walnuts.

3 Put the sugar, glucose syrup or golden syrup, salt and water in a heavy pan and place over a medium heat.

4 Stir to dissolve the sugar, then raise the heat. Boil the syrup until it reaches the firm-ball stage (120°C/248°F).

5 Meanwhile, place the egg white in a large, clean bowl and whisk until it forms firm peaks.

6 When the syrup is ready, pour it into the egg white, whisking constantly. Whip up into almost-firm peaks. Add the vanilla extract.

7 Whip up into almost-firm peaks again, then add the chopped walnuts and apricots and stir to combine.

8 Drop spoonfuls of the mixture on to the baking parchment or waxed paper. Leave to set up for about 20 minutes.

9 Serve either as they are or you could transfer them to mini paper cases if they are for a special occasion.

10 Store in an airtight container for up to 1 week.

VARIATION: If you want to omit the chopped apricots, use an extra 75g/3oz chopped walnuts instead.

Cherry divinity drops

The white swirls of meringue in these sweets are offset by the bright red of candied cherries. Use the best-quality candied cherries you can find, as they vary greatly in flavour. The vanilla and almond extract enhance the cherry flavour a little, but not enough to be cloying.

1 Line a baking sheet with baking parchment or waxed paper.

2 Chop 150g/5oz of the cherries into pieces, then slice the remaining 50g/2oz in half.

3 Put the sugar, glucose syrup, salt and water in a heavy pan and place over a medium heat.

4 Stir to dissolve the sugar and then raise the heat. Boil the syrup until it reaches the firm-ball stage (120°C/248°F).

5 Meanwhile, place the egg whites in a large, clean bowl and whisk until they form firm peaks.

6 When the syrup is ready, pour it into the whites, whisking constantly.

7 Whip up into almost-firm peaks, then add the vanilla and almond extracts. Whip up into almost-firm peaks again. Add the chopped cherries.

8 Put spoonfuls of the mixture on to the baking parchment or waxed paper, then place a halved cherry on top. Leave to set for about 20 minutes.

9 Serve either as they are or transfer to mini paper cases if they are for a special occasion. Store in an airtight container for up to 2 weeks.

makes: about 850g/1lb 14oz

200g/7oz candied cherries

400g/14oz/2 cups caster (superfine) sugar

120ml/4fl oz/½ cup glucose syrup

2.5ml/½ tsp salt

120ml/4fl oz/½ cup water

2 egg whites

2.5ml/½ tsp vanilla extract

2.5ml/½ tsp almond extract

Cook's Tip

Play around with the swirls of meringue by using two spoons to help slide the mixture from the spoon on to the baking parchment or waxed paper.

French nougat with candied fruit

makes: about 50 pieces

grapeseed or groundnut (peanut) oil, for greasing

rice paper

375g/13oz/scant 2 cups caster (superfine) sugar

25g/1oz glucose syrup or golden (light corn) syrup

100ml/3½fl oz/scant ½ cup water

350g/12oz honey

2 egg whites

300g/11oz good-quality candied fruit

100g/3¾oz whole almonds, lightly toasted

75g/3oz hazelnuts, lightly toasted

75g/3oz flaked (sliced) almonds, lightly toasted

75g/3oz pistachios, warmed

2.5ml/½ tsp fresh or dried lavender buds

a pinch of salt

40g/1½oz unsalted butter, cut into small pieces and softened

Cook's Tip

It is important to toast all of the nuts in this recipe separately. Hazelnuts and almonds need a bit of time in the oven, whereas pistachios simply require a few minutes.

There are two main types of nougat: white and brown. The white type is made with beaten egg whites and has a softer texture than the brown version, given here, which is made with added caramelized sugar. This recipe is for French nougat, which is thought to have originated in France in the 18th century. It is a wonderful contrast in tastes and texture, with soft, chewy nougat studded with crisp nuts and sweet, flavoursome candied fruit. Seek out top-quality candied fruits if you are not able to make them yourself. The food halls of department stores and fine delis will stock them at Christmas.

1 Grease a 15cm/6in square cake tin (pan) and line with the rice paper, or grease a baking sheet and line with rice paper to make a thinner nougat.

2 Put 350g/12oz/1¾ cups caster sugar, glucose syrup and water in a large, heavy pan and heat until the mixture reaches the soft-crack stage (143°C/290°F).

3 Warm the honey in a separate pan until it just bubbles, then add to the syrup and bring everything up to 143°C/290°F again.

4 Meanwhile, whisk the egg whites with the remaining 25g/1oz/2 tbsp of sugar until stiff peaks form.

5 Slowly pour the sugar and honey syrup into the whites in a stream and whisk until stiff and glossy. Tiny lumps may form, but don't worry and continue mixing.

6 Chop 100g/3¾oz of the candied fruit. Add to the nougat mixture with the toasted nuts, lavender buds and salt, and gently stir together.

7 Add the butter to the mixture and stir to combine thoroughly.

8 Spoon the nougat into the prepared tin or baking tray and smooth the top with an offset spatula or knife.

9 Decorate the surface of the nougat with large chunks or whole pieces of the remaining candied fruits.

10 Leave to set at room temperature for about 4–6 hours.

11 To remove the nougat from the tin, run an oiled paring knife around the edge and invert the cake tin, if using, or slip a metal offset spatula underneath the nougat if it is on a baking sheet.

12 Transfer to a chopping board. Cut into small pieces: diamonds look especially attractive. Serve immediately or store in an airtight container for about a week. Do not put the nougat in the refrigerator as this would make it soften and the colour from the fruit bleed on to the surface.

Pistachio nougat

Nougat is made slightly differently in every country. This is an Italian version, which is weighed down to make it slightly dense, but it is still gooey and light and the flavours of pistachio, honey and orange blossom water marry beautifully.

1 Grease a Swiss roll tin (jelly roll pan), then line with rice paper.

2 Put 350g/12oz/1¾ cups caster sugar, glucose syrup and water in a large, heavy pan and heat until the mixture reaches the soft-crack stage (143°C/290°F).

3 Warm the honey in a separate pan until it just boils, then add to the syrup and bring everything up to 143°C/290°F again.

4 Meanwhile, whisk the egg whites with the remaining 25g/1oz/2 tbsp sugar until stiff peaks form.

5 Slowly pour the sugar and honey syrup into the whites in a steady stream. Tiny lumps may form, but don't worry and continue mixing until the mixture is stiff and glossy.

6 Add the warm nuts and orange blossom water and gently fold together.

7 Pour the nougat into the prepared tin.

8 Cover the mixture with more sheets of rice paper and weigh down with a heavy board, such as a chopping board, and weights or dishes. If the chopping board smells strongly of e.g. onions, make sure you put it on a tray or place something in between it and the nougat or the nougat will take on the flavour of the onions. Leave to set for about 4 hours.

9 Remove the weights and board, turn out on to a chopping board and trim the sides to neaten them. Slice into bars or squares and serve. Store in an airtight container for about a week.

makes: about 1kg/2¼lb

grapeseed or groundnut (peanut) oil, for greasing

rice paper

375g/13oz/scant 2 cups caster (superfine) sugar

25g/1oz glucose syrup

100ml/3½fl oz/scant ½ cup water

175g/6oz honey

2 egg whites

250g/9oz whole almonds, lightly toasted

200g/7oz pistachios, warmed

5ml/1 tsp orange blossom water

Cook's Tip

Nougat varies around the world. In Spain it is firm and packed with nuts. The French weigh it down, but it is still soft and chewy. In the East it is more brittle and laced with blossom waters.

makes: 1 mouse

50g/2oz fondant per mouse
(see page 15)

a few drops of pink or brown food
colouring (optional)

coffee beans

silver balls or other decorations, for eyes

soft white string

inexpensive new pastry brush, to use
for whiskers (optional)

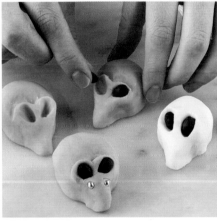

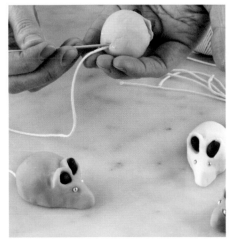

Sugar mice

Sugar mice are traditionally found in the Christmas stockings of British children.
They can be made from sugar set with egg whites or they can be formed from
soft sugar fondant, as here. The former is made much like a sugar egg, using
a mould. The latter can be made by hand and is a great project to do at home
with the kids. All kinds of sweets could be used to decorate the mice.

1 Wearing latex gloves, colour the
fondant either pink or brown, depending
what colour you want the mouse to be.
You could also leave the fondant white.
2 Shape the fondant into a pear shape
with a flat bottom. Carefully mould the
ears, using a sugar shaping tool or a
wooden skewer, to form indentations the
coffee beans can sit in. Push the coffee
beans into the ears.

3 Add silver balls or other decorations
for eyes. Add a ball for a nose, if you like.
4 Cut a length of string for the tail and
short pieces of the pastry brush for the
whiskers, if you like. Using sugar working
tools or a wooden skewer, push the
decorations into place.
5 Repeat to make as many mice as you
like, then allow them to dry completely
overnight at room temperature.

Sugar Easter egg

makes: 1 egg

400g/14oz/2 cups caster (superfine) sugar

2.5ml/½ tsp meringue powder

food colouring (optional)

cornflour (cornstarch), for dusting

45ml/3 tbsp egg whites or meringue powder

600g/1lb 6oz/5½ cups icing (confectioners') sugar

sugar decorations

For a child, looking inside a sugar Easter egg is like looking into a fairy tale. This recipe does require some patience, but the result is well worth the effort and makes a thoughtful alternative to a store-bought chocolate egg.

1   To make the egg, combine the sugar and meringue powder in a large bowl.

2   If you are colouring the egg, combine the desired amount of colour with 30ml/2 tbsp water and blend. Make a well in the sugar and add the water, and colouring, if using. Using a wooden spoon, stir to incorporate. It will have the consistency of wet sand.

3   Dust a two-piece plastic egg mould and a cake board or cardboard disc with cornflour. Using a spoon, press the sugar mixture into each half of the egg mould and pack it tightly to completely fill the moulds.

4   Using an offset metal spatula, scrape any excess sugar from the egg so that the surface is flush with the edge of the mould.

5   Unmould the mixture immediately by placing the cake board over the egg and inverting it. Remove the mould. Repeat with the other egg mould.

6   Decide how you want the egg oriented, then trim a small portion off either the bottom or the side of the egg for an upright or landscape egg. To do this, you can use a metal spatula or a length of thread. Saw 5mm/¼in off. You need to trim both halves of the egg, so place the halves next to each other with the side you are trimming facing you so they will match up.

7   Using a thread held taught between two hands, slice a piece from the rounded side of one half, leaving a window. Leave the cut-off portion resting on top of the egg so that the area inside does not dry out. Leave to dry for 1–1½ hours.

8   Meanwhile, prepare the royal icing. Combine the egg whites or meringue powder and icing sugar with 75ml/5 tbsp water in a large bowl. Using an electric mixer, beat for 8–10 minutes. The icing should form peaks. Add more water if needed.

9   Divide the icing into small bowls and colour each portion how you like. Cover with a damp cloth and set aside.

10 Carefully remove the sliced off portion of the egg and discard. Use a spoon to mark a 5mm/¼in rim around the opening. Scoop out the centre within these marks.

11 When you have dug out as much as you can, lift the egg up into the palm of your hand and turn it over so you can remove the remaining mixture through the cut off portion. Put it back down very carefully. You will now have a hollow egg half with a window on the curved edge.

12 Carefully pick up the other half of the egg and holding it in your hand, gently scoop out the centre, 5mm/¼in from the edge, following the contour of the egg. You should now have a hollow egg half.

13 Using your finger, smooth the opening on the inside of the egg halves. Place the egg halves right side-up on the cake boards and allow them to dry out for 24 hours.

14 Holding the egg halves in turn in the palm of your hand, file away any rough edges that remain using a clean emery board.

15 To decorate the egg, pipe icing clouds and grass on the inside of the hollow egg without the window. Pipe grass on the bottom inside of the half with the window. Leave the icing to set. Add your sugar decorations.

16 To join the two halves, squeeze icing around the flat rim of one egg half. Match the egg up with the other half and press together. Allow to dry for a few hours.

17 Pipe a trim around the edge of the window and the seam of the egg. Leave to set for a few more hours.

18 Store in an airtight container. Do not refrigerate. Present in a gift box, tied with a ribbon, if you like.

CANDIED FRUITS AND FLOWERS, AND JELLIED FRUITS

An excellent preservative, sugar is used in this chapter to transform fruit rinds, juices and purées into a range of stunning and sophisticated confections that are as pleasing to the eye as to the palate. From intense candied peel, pineapple and petals to flavourful jellies and pastes, and crisp slivers of pear, these jewel-like treats evoke memories of summer abundance and provide the perfect end to a special dinner.

Elegant, fruity and fun

Turning perfectly ripe fruits into charming confections requires a bit of time, a bit of sugar, a setting agent and a lot of friends to share them with. Adding sugar to fruit, its juices or its peel in specific amounts can completely change the intensity and texture, as well as helping to preserve it, and these confections make the perfect gift.

Candied citrus peel is a wonderful way of using up the skins of fruits after you have extracted the insides. The peel is repeatedly boiled in water and finally in a sugar syrup before being tossed in sugar and left to dry. It is an indispensable ingredient in the kitchen that can enhance so many sweets, desserts, muffins and cakes and, stored properly, it can last a year.

Whole or chopped fruits such as pineapple can be candied by a series of lengthy soaks in a sugar syrup. Each day the same syrup is reduced further to concentrate the flavour of the dehydrating fruit and extra sugar is added, until the syrup has completely replaced the fruit's own juices, producing a wonderfully sweet and soft sugary confection.

Old-fashioned gumdrops can be fashioned with a multitude of flavours and are set with gelatine and cornflour for a dense texture that demands something between chewing and sucking. Turkish delight is set with cornflour alone, and is one of the silkiest, softest confections made from fruit or flower extracts.

Fresh fruit juices can be set with gelatine and then cut into little bitesize pieces for serving. Fruit jellies will set with more clarity if a coarser sugar such as preserving sugar is used. Preserving sugar is also recommended as it dissolves more slowly, which helps prevent it burning.

Another way to set fruit for confections is with pectin. Much like making a jam, fruit pastes are a concentration of fruit that has been cooked for just the right amount of time. Depending on the natural pectins in the fruit, some pastes, such as quince, will need no additional setting agent. They will, however, need quite a long cooking time. Alternatively, fruits such as apples and pears can be thinly sliced, candied in syrup and baked for a crisp, translucent finish.

Candied citrus peel

Fresh candied citrus peel is far superior to any that you can buy, with a brighter colour and fresher flavour. There will be slight variances in the thickness and bitterness of different peels, so you will need to adjust the recipe accordingly.

1 Wash the fruit. Cut them in half and juice them. Reserve the juice for drinking or using in another recipe.

2 Put the peel in a pan and cover with cold water. Bring to the boil. Boil for 10 minutes.

3 Drain the peel, then return it to the pan and cover with fresh cold water. Bring to the boil again and drain. Repeat the blanching process a total of five times for grapefruit, three times for oranges and two times for clementines.

4 After the final blanching, test the tenderness of the peel by piercing it with the tip of a sharp knife. The knife should meet no resistance. If it still seems a little tough, blanch it once more.

5 Drain the peel and leave it until it is cool to the touch. Scrape away the soft pith using a spoon, then slice the peel into 1cm/½in strips with a sharp knife.

6 Put the granulated sugar and water in a clean pan. Stir over a medium heat to dissolve the sugar.

7 Add the peel, stop stirring and bring the syrup to a boil. Boil for 45 minutes, or until the syrup reduces and bubbles form (about 110°C/225°F). The peel will become slightly translucent. Leave to cool overnight.

8 Remove the peel from the syrup with a slotted spoon and lay it out on a wire rack placed over a piece of baking parchment to catch the drips. Leave it to dry for 24 hours.

9 The next day, touch the peel to see if it is almost dry. If it is too moist the sugar you toss it in will dissolve, but if it is too dry the sugar will not adhere to the peel. When it is just tacky, toss the strips in the caster sugar, spread out on the wire rack and leave to dry for a few hours. Store in an airtight container for up to 6 months.

makes: about 1.2kg/2½lb

3 grapefruits, 4 oranges, or 12 clementines, preferably organic

800g/1¾lb/4 cups granulated (white) sugar

400ml/14fl oz/1⅔ cups water

100g/3¾oz/½ cup caster (superfine) sugar

Cook's Tip

If the peel is thicker and more bitter, blanch it for longer to soften it and remove more of the bitter oils.

Candied stem ginger

Peppery, sweet and aromatic, these golden chunks of candied ginger in syrup are a real treat. It is important to select heavy, plump-looking stem ginger. If the root is at all shrivelled, it will not have that spiciness that it needs to balance out the sweetness of this process.

makes: about 1kg/2¼lb

300g/11oz fresh root ginger

500g/1¼lb/2½ cups granulated (white) sugar

550ml/18fl oz/2½ cups water

15ml/1 tbsp glucose syrup

1 Peel the ginger and cut it into 2cm/¾in chunks. Try to cut the chunks with the shape of the root rather than against it, so you get some nice little bulbous shapes.

2 Place the prepared ginger in a pan and cover with cold water. Bring to the boil and cook for 20 minutes.

3 Drain, then return the ginger to the pan and cover with fresh cold water. Bring to the boil again and drain. Repeat the blanching process a total of four times.

4 Place the sugar, water and glucose syrup into a clean pan (do not reuse the pot you blanched the ginger in without washing it, or the syrup could crystallize).

5 Stir over a medium heat to dissolve the sugar. Once dissolved, stop stirring and bring to the boil. Boil for about 45 minutes until the ginger becomes translucent.

6 Leave the candied ginger to cool in the syrup overnight.

7 Remove the ginger from the syrup with a slotted spoon and place it in a sterilized jar. Pour syrup over the fruit to cover it completely and store in the refrigerator.

8 Alternatively, you could strain the ginger and lay it on a wire rack to dry overnight. The next day, toss in granulated sugar and lay out on a wire rack again to dry for a few hours.

Candied pineapple

makes: about 1.2kg/2½lb

1 pineapple

about 1kg/2¼lb granulated (white) or caster (superfine) sugar

liquid glucose

Cook's Tip

The sweet taste of pineapple deepens and becomes more concentrated in this recipe, because you replace the water content in the fruit with a reduced pineapple sugar syrup.

Although this recipe takes a long time (about two weeks) to prepare, the end result is golden-glazed candied pineapple that is unlike any other candied fruit. It makes a really special gift, or can be used in many festive recipes.

1 Using a large, sharp knife, cut off the top and base of the pineapple. Stand the pineapple upright and, working in a circular motion to retain the shape of the pineapple, carefully cut the skin off, starting at the top and finishing at the bottom of the fruit.

2 Slice the pineapple into round discs about 1cm/½in thick. Using a small paring knife, cut out the hard inner core.

3 Weigh the fruit and measure 250ml/8fl oz/ 1 cup water per 500g/1¼lb fruit. Put the water into a large pan.

4 Place the fruit gently in the water and cook over a medium heat for 15 minutes, until it is tender but not falling apart. Position a wire rack over a baking sheet and, with a slotted spoon, transfer the pineapple to the rack to drain. Reserve the liquid.

5 For every 250ml/8fl oz/1 cup of the reserved cooking liquid, add 150g/5oz/ ¾ cup sugar and 15ml/1 tbsp liquid glucose. Place the pan over a moderate heat and stir until the sugar dissolves. Bring to the boil.

6 Place the fruit in a large roasting pan in a single layer. Pour the boiling syrup over the pineapple to submerge it completely.

7 Cover with baking parchment or waxed paper and press down slightly. Set aside for 24 hours.

8 The following day, remove the paper, transfer the fruit to a wire rack and measure the remaining syrup. Pour the syrup into a heavy pan with an additional 50g/2oz sugar for every 300ml/½ pint/1¼ cups syrup. Bring to the boil.

9 Place the fruit back into the roasting pan and cover with the hot syrup. Cover with baking parchment or waxed paper again, pressing down. Leave for another 24 hours.

10 Repeat steps 8 and 9 for five more days.

11 On the eighth day, add 75g/3oz sugar for every 300ml/½ pint/1¼ cups of syrup, then let the fruit steep for 48 hours.

12 On the tenth day add 75g/3oz sugar for every 300ml/½ pint/1¼ cups of syrup, then let the fruit steep for four more days.

13 Transfer the fruit to a wire rack set over a tray. Preheat the oven to 110°C/225°F/Gas ¼. Put the tray in the oven, turn off the heat and leave for at least four hours.

14 Serve immediately, or store in a container in the refrigerator for up to six months.

unsprayed, fragrant garden roses

egg white

caster (superfine) sugar

Crystallized rose petals

If you have beautiful, fragrant roses growing in your garden you are very fortunate indeed! This is a wonderful use of the petals when you have a glut of flowers in the late spring and early summer, and the crystallized petals make a sweet decoration for desserts or cakes, or a glass of champagne.

1 Position sheets of baking parchment underneath cooling racks on a work surface, to catch the sugar.

2 Gently separate the rose petals from the flowers, one rose at a time. Keep the other roses in water.

3 Very lightly, brush the petals, a few at a time, with egg white, using a fine, new paintbrush.

4 You don't need to dip the brush into the egg wash each time, as only a thin coating is required to make the sugar adhere.

5 Sprinkle the painted petals with sugar and gently place on a cooling rack to dry. Leave to dry for 24–36 hours.

6 Serve immediately or store in an airtight container. The colour and flavour will fade, so enjoy them within a month.

Turkish delight

This fresh version of a sweet-shop classic tastes very different from many commercially produced versions, so it is worth trying even if you think you don't like it. The texture is soft and silky, and the aroma of perfumed roses with a hint of lemon makes these fragrant treats a real delight.

1 Grease an 18cm/7in square tin (pan).
2 Put the sugar, 150ml/¼ pint/⅔ cup of the water and the cream of tartar into a heavy pan. Stir to dissolve the sugar, then bring to the boil and heat until it reaches the soft-ball stage (114°C/238°F). Set aside.
3 Combine the cornflour, icing sugar and 50ml/2fl oz/¼ cup of the water in a small, heatproof bowl to make a paste.
4 Boil the remaining 700ml/1 pint 3½fl oz/ scant 3 cups of the water and pour over the cornflour paste, whisking to dissolve. Return to the pan and simmer until clear and thick.
5 Gradually start adding the sugar syrup to the pan, whisking constantly. Boil for a further 30 minutes.

6 The mixture should be a pale yellow colour and be rather transparent.
7 Add the honey and add rose water and lemon extract to taste. Add a few drops of pink food colouring and combine.
8 Pour the mixture into the tin. Leave to cool completely for several hours.
9 Turn the Turkish delight out on to a board that has been dusted generously with icing sugar. Cut into cubes and toss in more icing sugar. You may need to repeat this if it absorbs a lot of the sugar.
10 Pack into boxes or containers with a generous amount of icing sugar to stop it sticking. Serve immediately or store in an airtight container for up to a week. Dust with more sugar if needed.

makes: about 1.6kg/3½lb

butter, for greasing

450g/1lb/2¼ cups caster (superfine) sugar

900ml/1½ pints/3¾ cups water

2.5ml/½ tsp cream of tartar

75g/3oz/⅔ cup cornflour (cornstarch)

200g/7oz/generous 1⅓ cups icing (confectioners') sugar, plus extra for dusting

50g/2oz honey

rose water

lemon extract

pink food colouring

Pineapple chews

You can use home-made candied pineapple or good-quality store-bought candied pineapple to make these fruity morsels. The rum adds a lovely depth to the chews and cuts the sweetness. Be sure to use a white rum, as dark, spiced rum would overwhelm the pineapple flavour.

1 Grease an 18cm/7in square baking tin (pan) and line with baking parchment or waxed paper.

2 Put the butter, sugar and milk in a heavy pan. Cook over moderate heat, stirring, until the sugar dissolves completely.

3 Bring the mixture to the boil and cook until it reaches the soft-ball stage (114°C/238°F). Remove from the heat.

4 Add the chopped candied pineapple, white chocolate, lemon juice and rum.

5 Leave the mixture to cool slightly, then give it two stirs and leave it for 1–2 minutes to cool a bit further.

6 Stir twice again, then leave for 1–2 minutes. Continue in this way, allowing it to cool down slightly between stirs. As it cools, the mixture will get thicker.

7 Transfer the mixture to the tin and press down the surface with an offset spatula.

8 Press the candied pineapple wedges onto the surface, making sure they are evenly spaced, in rows of six. Score the surface with a sharp knife so that there are 36 pieces with a pineapple wedge in the centre. Leave to set completely.

9 Cut it into 36 pieces and serve. Store in an airtight container.

makes: 36 chews

25g/1oz/2 tbsp unsalted butter, plus extra for greasing

300g/11oz/1½ cups caster (superfine) sugar

120ml/4fl oz/½ cup full-fat (whole) milk

185g/6½oz Candied Pineapple (see page 104), chopped, plus 50g/2oz Candied Pineapple, cut into 36 small wedges

25g/1oz white chocolate, chopped

2.5ml/½ tsp lemon juice

2.5ml/½ tsp white rum

makes: about 800g/1¾lb

water or oil, for greasing

20g/¾oz powdered gelatine

100ml/3½fl oz/scant ½ cup cold water

400g/14oz/2 cups caster (superfine) sugar

100ml/3½fl oz/scant ½ cup hot water

15ml/1 tbsp lemon juice

100g/3¾oz candied ginger,
finely chopped

50g/2oz/½ cup cornflour (cornstarch)

50g/2oz/½ cup icing (confectioners') sugar

Cook's Tip
It is useful to have a dish of hot water to hand to dip the cutter into occasionally. This will help prevent the cutter from sticking to the gumdrops and give a cleaner finish.

Ginger gumdrops

Gumdrops are dense and chewy. They can be made in an assortment of colours and flavours. These are made with spicy candied ginger, which creates a gumdrop with a little bite. The texture of the ginger contrasts well with the gummy sweet and together they form a delicious treat.

1 Sprinkle a 20cm/8in square cake tin (pan) with water or lightly grease it with oil and line it with clear film. Set aside.
2 Put the gelatine in a small bowl and add the cold water. Stir to dissolve.
3 Put the sugar and hot water in a pan, stir to dissolve, then bring to the boil. Boil for 10 minutes.
4 Add the soaked gelatine and boil for a further 15 minutes.

5 Add the lemon juice and ginger, remove from the heat and leave to cool slightly. Pour into the tin. Leave to set for 24 hours.
6 Turn the mixture out on to a board. Cut into small rounds with a tiny cookie cutter. Transfer to a cooling rack and allow to dry for a couple of hours.
7 Dust all over with a mixture of the cornflour and icing sugar, then serve. Store in an airtight container.

Two-tone fruit jellies

makes: about 30–40 small pieces

350g/12oz strawberries

350g/12oz apricots

butter, for greasing

500g/1¼lb/2½ cups preserving sugar

75ml/5 tbsp glucose syrup or golden (light corn) syrup

150ml/¼ pint/⅔ cup water

0.75ml/1⅛ tsp cream of tartar

15g/½oz powdered pectin or 65g/2½oz liquid pectin

10ml/2 tsp lemon juice

100g/3¾oz/½ cup granulated (white) sugar, for coating

This stunning two-toned treat is made from two differently flavoured layers of silky, springy jelly. Half tangy apricot, half sweet strawberry, these jellies taste as good as they look and are a great way of using up overripe fruits.

1 Put the fruit in separate pans with 30ml/2 tbsp water in each and cook for about 10 minutes until soft and releasing their juices. Purée each mixture separately in a blender or food processor. Put in separate bowls and set aside.

2 Lightly grease a 15cm/6in square tin (pan). Line with clear film (plastic wrap), making the film as smooth as possible.

3 In a small bowl, stir 25g/1oz/2 tbsp of the preserving sugar into the strawberry purée and another 25g/1oz/2 tbsp of the preserving sugar into the apricot purée. Set aside.

4 In a large, heavy pan, mix the remaining sugar with the glucose syrup or golden syrup, water and cream of tartar. Place over a low heat, stirring until the sugar dissolves.

5 Stop stirring, turn the heat up to medium and bring to the boil. When it reaches a rolling boil, turn the heat up to high. Boil, without stirring, until the syrup reaches 130°C/266°F.

6 Mix half the pectin into the strawberry purée mixture and the other half into the apricot mixture. Put the apricot mixture into a clean heavy pan and pour half of the boiled syrup over it.

7 Add the strawberry mixture to the pan containing the remaining boiled syrup. Gently stir each to combine, but then stop stirring. Boil, without stirring, until the temperature goes back up to 103°C/217°F.

8 Add 5ml/1 tsp lemon juice to each pan and continue boiling until the mixtures reach 106°C/223°F

9 Give the strawberry mixture a stir, just before pouring it into the prepared tin. Leave to cool for 10 minutes. Now pour the apricot mixture over the top. Leave overnight at room temperature, uncovered.

10 Lift the jelly out of the tin by taking hold of the edges of the clear film and transferring the jelly to a chopping board. Peel off the clear film.

11 Cut into little squares or shapes and dip in sugar. Lay them out on baking parchment to dry for about an hour. Store them in an airtight container for about a week.

VARIATION: You can have fun playing around with flavour combinations. Orange and passionfruit or elderflower and rhubarb are good. Substitute equal parts of juices, cordials or purées to create your perfect two-tone jellies.

Blackberry paste

A fruit paste has more of a jammy consistency and a more concentrated flavour than a fruit jelly. They are a wonderful confection for capturing the essence of seasonal fruits. This recipe is for fruits that contain very little natural pectin, such as berries and plums.

makes: about 30–40 small pieces

800g/1¾lb blackberries

butter, for greasing

500g/1¼lb/2½ cups preserving sugar

75ml/5 tbsp glucose syrup or golden (light corn) syrup

150ml/¼ pint/⅔ cup water

0.75ml/1⅛ tsp cream of tartar

15g/½oz powdered pectin or 65g/2½oz liquid pectin

10ml/2 tsp lemon juice

100g/3¾oz/½ cup granulated (white) sugar, for coating

1 Put the blackberries in a heavy pan and heat gently until the fruits soften and the juices run. Do not stir.

2 Strain through a sieve (strainer) placed over a large bowl. Push the fruit through with the back of a spoon. You should have about 500ml/17fl oz/ generous 2 cups purée. Discard the seeds left in the sieve.

3 Lightly grease a 15cm/6in square tin (pan). Line with clear film (plastic wrap), making the film as smooth as possible.

4 In a small bowl, stir 50g/2oz/¼ cup of the preserving sugar into the blackberry purée and set aside.

5 In a large, heavy pan, mix the remaining sugar with the glucose syrup or golden syrup, water and cream of tartar. Place over a low heat, stirring until the sugar dissolves.

6 Stop stirring, turn the heat up to medium and bring to the boil. When it reaches a rolling boil, turn the heat up to high. Boil, without stirring, until the syrup reaches 130°C/266°F.

7 Mix the pectin into the blackberry purée mixture. Add to the boiling syrup and stir gently to combine.

8 Boil, without stirring, until the temperature goes back up to 103°C/217°F.

9 Add the lemon juice and continue boiling until it reaches 106°C/223°F.

10 Give the syrup a stir at this point, just before pouring it into the prepared tin. Leave to cool overnight at room temperature, uncovered.

11 Lift the paste out of the tin by taking hold of the edges of the clear film and transferring the paste to a chopping board. Peel off the clear film.

12 Cut the paste into little squares or use a cutter to create shapes, such as hearts or stars.

13 Dip the shapes in granulated sugar. Dip your fingers in sugar regularly as you work so they don't stick to the paste and break it.

14 Lay the paste shapes out on parchment paper and leave to dry for about an hour.

15 Serve immediately or store in an airtight container, in the refrigerator, for up to a week

Quince paste

Quince must be cooked in order to bring out its delicious flavour and deep jewel colouring. It is most often served in the form of a paste. The Spanish call it membrillo and serve it with sheep's milk cheese. It is also made and presented at French and Mexican tables.

makes: about 60 small squares

butter, for greasing

4 or 5 large quinces

100ml/3½fl oz/scant ½ cup water

about 1.2kg/2½lb/6 cups granulated (white) or preserving sugar

45ml/3 tbsp fresh lemon juice, strained

1 Butter a baking tray or a Swiss roll tin (jelly roll pan) and line the base and sides with baking parchment.

2 Wash the quinces well to remove any fuzz. Quarter the fruit and core, but leave the peel on. Cut into smaller chunks and place the fruit in a large, heavy pan.

3 Add the water, cover the pan and simmer over a low heat for about 1 hour, or until the fruit is soft and tender. Stir occasionally. Add more water if necessary.

4 Remove the pan from the heat. Pass the fruit through a food mill or sieve (strainer). Weigh the fruit pulp and place back into the pan. Measure an equal weight of sugar and stir it into the puréed quince.

5 Place the pan over a very low heat and stirring, occasionally, cook for about 1½–2 hours until the paste is a dark garnet colour.

6 Test the mixture by putting a spoonful on a plate. It should firm up and, when it cools, it should be matte and not sticky.

7 Stir in the lemon juice.

8 Spread the mixture in the prepared baking tray or Swiss roll tin and leave to cool. This may take a couple of hours.

9 Once cooled, cut the paste into shapes or use a cutter. Roll in sugar.

10 Serve immediately or store in an airtight container in the refrigerator for up to 3 weeks.

Baked pear crisps

Lightly poaching slices of pear in sugar syrup then drying them out in the oven transforms the delicate texture of a fresh pear into a crisp, sweet treat. They become slightly translucent in the process, making them look a little like stained glass. They are also wonderful dipped into chocolate.

1 Line a baking sheet with baking parchment. Preheat the oven to 110°C/225°F/Gas ¼.

2 Slice the pears paper-thin on a mandolin or with a very sharp thin-bladed knife and immediately squeeze lime or lemon juice over them to prevent them from turning brown and to add flavour.

3 Combine the sugar and water in a heavy pan and heat over a medium heat to dissolve. Once the sugar is fully dissolved, turn up the heat and bring to the boil. Cook until the syrup reaches the thread stage (111°C/233°F).

4 Place the pear slices in the reduced syrup (you can do this in two batches) and cook for 2 minutes.

5 Lift the slices from the syrup with a slotted spoon, draining off as much of the syrup as possible.

6 Lay the slices out evenly on the prepared baking sheet and put them in the preheated oven.

7 Bake for 2 hours then, using a spatula, flip the slices over and bake for a further 20 minutes, until completely dry.

8 Leave to cool, then serve. Store in an airtight container for up to 2 weeks.

makes: about 20 crisps

2 underripe pears, such as Comice

juice of 2 limes or lemons

400g/14oz/2 cups caster (superfine) sugar

200ml/7fl oz/scant 1 cup water

MARZIPAN, NUT CONFECTIONS AND LIQUORICE

Nuts are a key ingredient in sweet-making. With their many types and flavours, they add nuance and texture to recipes. Simple nut pastes can be cooked and moulded by hand as well as being mixed with orange zest and coated with melted chocolate, sandwiched between hazelnuts or stuffed into dates. Liquorice root or anise is the key to intensely flavoured drops, brittle shards, and chewy sticks, and the range on offer will please even the most ardent liquorice-lover.

Nutty, versatile and intense

This chapter contains some of the easiest and some of the most challenging confections to make at home. Nut pastes are easy and fast. If you want to get creative, they can be time-consuming and slightly fiddly, but they are not difficult. Liquorice sweets, on the other hand, can take time to get the hang of.

To make nut pastes, little is required other than combining nuts with some liquid and sugar, and the possibilities are limitless when it comes to shape and flavour. The simplest nut paste is bound together with egg whites and icing sugar, and used as an ingredient in baking. Almost any combination of nuts can be used, but there should always be a proportion of ground almonds for structure. Baking nut paste will yield a crisp outer shell and gooey centre, which can then be sandwiched with jam or adorned with candied fruits.

A smoother, more pliable nut paste results from cooking a combination of nuts, sugar and egg whites on the stove. Cooked nut paste is what is generally known as marzipan and can be coloured and shaped in countless ways. Marzipan dipped in chocolate is a quick and delicious after-dinner treat, or it can be mixed with coarsely chopped nuts and dropped in brewed espresso, orange zest or bitter almond extract for a more sophisticated yet equally simple confection. If you have lots of time, get creative with marzipan bumblebees, or miniature fruits and vegetables.

At the other end of the spectrum lies liquorice. Deep flavours of black treacle, liquorice root, star anise, aniseed and, sometimes, sweetened condensed milk can be boiled together to a dark bubbly mass. The original flavour of true liquorice comes from the root of the same name. Star anise, anise, and fennel have similar taste sensations, but are not related botanically.

There are many varieties of black liquorice, from the sweetest chewy-soft pieces to the hardest, saltiest drops. Whichever you fancy, be prepared to watch the pan closely – one false move and the whole thing can burn. Follow the recipes carefully, however, and you will be able to create your own home-made classics.

Simple almond paste

The simplest nut paste is one made with nuts, sugar and egg. You can alter the flavour and texture by using different nuts in varied proportions, but it is usually most successful if you use at least some ground almonds, in combination with another type of ground nut for flavour. Almond paste is a wonderful ingredient for using in cakes and cookies.

1 Combine the ground almonds and icing sugar in a large bowl.
2 In a small bowl, use a fork or small whisk to beat the egg white until frothy.
3 Slowly add the beaten egg white to the almond and sugar mixture, stirring until it just comes together. You may not need all of the egg white.
4 Add the bitter almond oil, if using.

5 Knead the mixture lightly until it is smooth and holds together. Avoid over-kneading, as it will cause the mixture to become brittle.
6 Use the paste according to the recipe. To store, wrap it in two layers of clear film (plastic wrap). Keep in an airtight container in the refrigerator for up to 2 weeks. You can freeze it for up to 3 months.

makes: about 500g/1¼lb

200g/7oz ground almonds

300g/11oz/2⅔ cups icing (confectioners') sugar

1 egg white

2 drops bitter almond oil (optional)

Cook's Tip
You can grind skinned, whole almonds in a coffee grinder if you are uncertain of the freshness of pre-ground almonds.

Boiled marzipan

Cooked nut pastes are made in much the same way as simple nut pastes, but the heat changes the texture of the finished product significantly. These types of nut pastes are ideal for rolling and using for covering cakes, and for shaping. You can further alter the flavour and texture of a nut paste by using different nuts and varied proportions, so long as you use some ground almonds.

1 Heat the sugar and water in a heavy pan over a medium heat until the sugar dissolves.
2 Once the sugar has dissolved, increase the heat and bring the mixture to the soft-ball stage (114°C/238°F).
3 Dip the base of the pan in an ice-water bath to arrest the cooking.
4 Add the ground almonds and stir. Stir in the egg white and return to the heat.
5 Stir for a short while over a low heat, until the marzipan thickens slightly. Remove from the heat. Leave to cool slightly.

6 Turn out the mixture on to a clean, dry work surface dusted with icing sugar. Knead gently for about 5–6 minutes until it is smooth and holds together.
7 Add a few drops of food colouring and/or flavouring, if using, and knead in to distribute evenly.
8 Use the paste according to the recipe. To store, wrap it tightly in two layers of clear film (plastic wrap). Keep in an airtight container in the refrigerator for up to 2 weeks. You can freeze it for up to 3 months.

makes: about 600g/1lb 6oz

300g/11oz/1½ cups caster (superfine) sugar
150ml/¼ pint/⅔ cup water
200g/7oz/1 cup ground almonds
1 egg white, slightly beaten
icing (confectioners') sugar, for kneading
colouring or flavouring, optional

Cook's Tip
It is best to allow the marzipan to cool slightly before attempting to roll it out, if you use it for covering a cake.

Marzipan bumblebees

These cute little bees will be a hit with children, and are the perfect decoration for cupcakes or a birthday cake. Make the marzipan a day in advance and leave it to mature overnight at room temperature before colouring and shaping it into bees. This will make it easier to work with and it will hold its shape better.

1 Divide the marzipan into two pieces and colour half yellow and half black.
2 Divide each colour into four pieces. Roll each of these out into logs about 5mm/¼in in diameter, so you have four yellow logs and four black logs. Cover any that you are not working with with clear film (plastic wrap). Cut each log into 5mm/¼in pieces.
3 Alternating the colours, sandwich together three pieces, two yellow and one black, to resemble the body of a bee.

4 To make the heads, roll a black piece into a ball and press it into the body. To make the eyes, push two yellow, black or white hundreds and thousands into the head.
5 To make the wings, choose the most perfect flaked almonds and push them gently into the body to create two wings.
6 Serve immediately, or store at room temperature covered with clear film or in an airtight container. Do not refrigerate or the flaked almonds will soften and the colour of the hundreds and thousands will bleed.

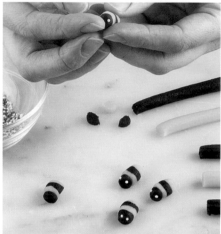

makes: about 10 bees

150g/5oz Boiled Marzipan (*see* page 121) or use good store-bought marzipan

a few drops of yellow and black food colouring

hundreds and thousands (sprinkles)

flaked (sliced) almonds

makes: 24 balls

200g/7oz Boiled Marzipan (*see* page 121)
or use good store-bought marzipan

zest of one orange

100g/3¾oz dark (bittersweet) chocolate

chocolate or coloured sprinkles

Orange-almond morsels

These sweet little marzipan balls draped in chocolate are the perfect treat for lovers of chocolate and orange. Because they are small, and covered in chocolate sprinkles, these will appeal to children, although they may prefer milk chocolate, which, of course, you could use instead.

1 Place the marzipan on a board, place the orange zest on top and knead until the zest is evenly incorporated.

2 Roll the marzipan into a log about 2cm/¾in thick. Cut 2cm/¾in pieces from the log and roll each piece into a ball.

3 Melt the chocolate in a heat-proof bowl over barely simmering water. Put the sprinkles in a small bowl. Lay individual doilies out on a pretty tray.

4 Dip one end of each ball of marzipan into the melted chocolate, then dip that into the sprinkles. Transfer to the prepared doilies.

5 Allow the chocolate to set before serving. Uncoated orange-almond balls will keep for two weeks in an airtight container in the refrigerator. Once they are dipped in chocolate they should be eaten within a few days.

200g/7oz Boiled Marzipan (*see* page 121) or use good store-bought marzipan

50g/2oz hazelnuts, toasted and chopped

25ml/1½ tbsp cold espresso or strong coffee

5ml/1 tsp fresh espresso grounds

2.5ml/½ tsp cognac or Grand Marnier

caster (superfine) sugar, for rolling

Espresso-hazelnut balls

Marzipan is a wonderful vehicle for other flavours. The bitterness of good fresh coffee or espresso grounds together with the warmth of toasted hazelnuts is always a good combination. Adding alcohol can also help to cut the sweetness, making these the perfect accompaniment to coffee after a special dinner.

1   Put all of the ingredients except the caster sugar into a large bowl and mix together with clean hands.

2   Divide the mixture into 24 pieces and roll into balls.

3   Pour some sugar on to a plate and roll the balls around in it – you will need to do this in a couple of batches.

4   Serve immediately, or store, covered, for up to 2 weeks in the refrigerator.

Marzipan-stuffed hazelnuts

These adorable little bites of toasted hazelnuts sandwiched around orange flavoured marzipan make a sweet end to any meal. They take a little time to assemble, but it is a very simple recipe, so you could enlist help from children.

1 Line a baking sheet with baking parchment and preheat the oven to 160°C/325°F/Gas 3.

2 Spread out the hazelnuts in an even layer and place in the middle of the oven to bake for about 7 minutes. Check the nuts periodically as they can burn quickly. They should be golden brown on the outside.

3 Meanwhile, put the marzipan and orange or clementine juice and zest in a small bowl and knead together with your hands or the back of a spoon.

4 When the nuts are sufficiently toasted, empty them on to a clean dish towel and remove the skins by rubbing them together through the towel.

5 Shake off any excess skin and, using a paring knife, split the nuts in half along their seams. Leave to cool completely.

6 Roll the marzipan filling into about 40 tiny balls and use to sandwich two hazelnut halves together.

7 Dust with cocoa powder and icing sugar. Serve immediately or store in an airtight container in a cool place for up to two weeks.

VARIATION: Whole almonds or walnuts will also work well. Just remember to adjust the toasting time for the nuts. Walnuts need only have the slightest tinge of yellow-gold whereas the hazelnuts should be golden-brown.

makes: about 40 balls

150g/5oz large, whole hazelnuts with skins on (the biggest ones you can find)

200g/7oz Boiled Marzipan (*see* page 121) or use good store-bought marzipan

juice and zest of 1 orange or clementine

cocoa powder and icing (confectioners') sugar, for dusting

Stuffed dates

Originating in north Africa, dates stuffed with nut paste have long been a festive treat in the Middle East and Mediterranean. Pistachios and dates have a natural affinity, since they grow in the same areas, and the combination is further enhanced in this delectable recipe by the inclusion of marzipan, orange zest and candied peel. These make an ideal alternative to chocolates at Christmas.

1 Prepare the dates by slitting them down one side and removing the stones (pits) with the tip of a knife, leaving a cavity for the stuffing.

2 Combine the marzipan, Kirsch, and orange zest in a bowl and mix well using clean hands.

3 Separate the marzipan into 12 pieces and roll into little balls. Wash your hands.

4 Press a marzipan ball into the centre of each date and gently squeeze the date around the filling to create an even shape.

5 Chop the pistachios finely and sprinkle over the dates. Press in a piece of candied peel, if you like.

6 Place each date in a little sweet case. Serve immediately or store, covered, for up to two weeks in the refrigerator.

makes: 12 stuffed dates

12 dates, preferably Barhi or Medjool

115g/4oz Boiled Marzipan (*see* page 121) or use good store-bought marzipan

15ml/1 tbsp Kirsch

zest from 1 orange

15–20 pistachios

candied orange peel (optional)

Cook's Tip
The best dates for this recipe have papery, sheer skin surrounding a sticky and soft caramel-like flesh.

makes: 30–35 stars

100g/3¾oz/scant 1 cup ground almonds

100g/3¾oz/generous ½ cup granulated (white) sugar

1 egg white

10ml/2 tsp Kirsch

15–18 Amarena cherries

Cook's Tip
If you make bigger biscuits (cookies), cook them for slightly longer. They should be golden-brown.

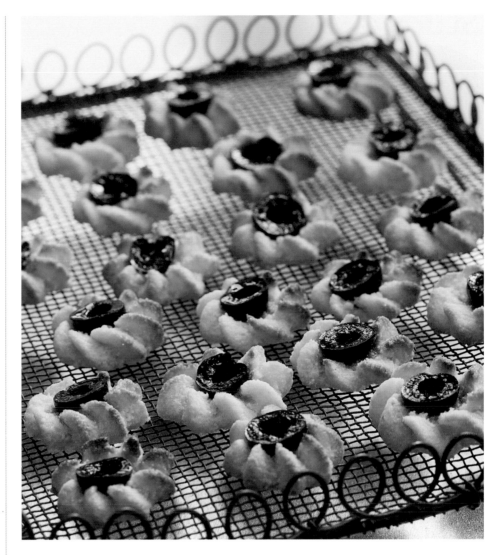

Cherry-almond stars

Amarena cherries are a wild Italian variety of the fruit. They are very sour straight from the tree, but they are usually stoned and immediately packed in sugar in jars. The sugar macerates the cherries and extracts their natural juices, creating a delicious syrup and intense sweet-and-sour cherry. In this recipe they are combined with crumbly, buttery almond biscuits to create a taste sensation.

1 Line a baking sheet with baking parchment and heat the oven to 180°C/350°F/Gas 4.

2 Combine the ground almonds, sugar, egg white, and Kirsch in a bowl with a wooden spoon.

3 Fit a piping (pastry) bag with a star tip and fill it with the mixture. Pipe the mixture into little stars.

4 Halve the cherries through the hole where they have been stoned rather than halving them through the stem. Put one half, cut side up, on top of each star.

5 Put the stars in the pre-heated oven and bake for about 7 minutes, until golden. Leave to cool completely, then serve.

6 These will keep for a couple of days in an airtight container at room temperature.

Liquorice shards

This is a hard version of liquorice, to suck on rather than chew. The bicarbonate of soda lightens the texture a bit, so the shards are slightly brittle. Liquorice roots are available in most health food shops and in some traditional sweet shops as well. If you can't find them, you could use a star anise pod instead, which is easier to find in larger supermarkets.

1 Grease a 23cm/9in square cake tin (pan) and line with clear film (plastic wrap).
2 Combine the sugar, syrup, black treacle, water and cream of tartar in a heavy pan. Stir over a low heat to dissolve. Add the liquorice root and boil until it reaches 120°C/265°F.
3 In a separate bowl, combine the pectin (add 60ml/4 tbsp water if using powdered pectin), bicarbonate of soda and salt.

4 Pour the pectin mixture into the syrup and stir to combine. This will lower the temperature of the syrup slightly. Boil again until the syrup reaches 103°C/217°F, then stir in the anise extract.
5 Pour the syrup into the prepared tin and allow it to set for about 4 hours. Turn out on to a board and break into shapes.
6 Serve immediately or store in an airtight container for up to 3 weeks.

butter, for greasing

200g/7oz/1 cup caster (superfine) sugar

100g/3¾oz golden (light corn) syrup

100g/3¾oz black treacle (molasses)

100ml/3½fl oz/scant ½ cup water

2.5ml/½ tsp cream of tartar

1 liquorice root, pounded

65g/2½oz liquid fruit pectin or 12g/¼oz powdered fruit pectin

2.5ml/½ tsp bicarbonate of soda (baking soda)

2.5ml/½ tsp salt

5ml/1 tsp anise extract

Pontefract cakes

These soft liquorice cakes are from Pontefract, England, and date back to 1614. Originally a seal with a depiction of Pontefract Castle was applied to the top of each cake by hand. It's fun to be creative and create your own seal or pattern. If you have some little madeleine, tartlet or jelly moulds, try using the bottom of those, or if you have a wax seal stamp with your initial on it, use that.

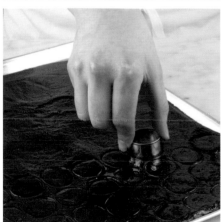

1 Grease a 23 x 33cm/9 x 13in baking tray and set aside.

2 Place all of the ingredients in a heavy pan and heat gently, stirring, until the sugar is dissolved.

3 Turn up the heat and bring the syrup up to 112°C/233°F, stirring constantly, without scraping down the sides of pan.

4 Pour the mixture into the prepared tray.

5 Place in the refrigerator to cool for about 10 minutes.

6 Remove it from the refrigerator and turn out on to a work surface. Stamp out small rounds with a cutter. Press the tops of the cakes with the stamp or mould.

7 Serve immediately, or wrap in waxed paper and store in an airtight container for up to 1 month.

makes: about 550g/1lb 6oz

100g/3¾oz butter, plus extra for greasing

200g/7oz/1 cup caster (superfine) sugar

75ml/5 tbsp golden (light corn) syrup

45ml/3 tbsp black treacle (molasses)

120ml/8tbsp sweetened condensed milk

2.5ml/½ tsp of salt

7.5ml/1½ tsp anise extract

a few drops black food colouring

5ml/1 tsp bicarbonate of soda (baking soda)

Liquorice sticks

A favourite with children and adults everywhere, liquorice sticks are delectable on their own, or you could dip them in sherbet. You can make these the traditional way with anise extract and black food colouring, or you could make red liquorice and omit the anise.

1   Line a 23cm/9in square baking tin (pan) with foil. Extend the foil over the edges of the tin. Butter the foil.

2   Melt the butter in a large, heavy pan. Add the sugar, sweetened condensed milk, golden syrup and salt. Stir well to combine.

3   Boil the mixture at a steady, moderate rate over a medium heat, stirring often, until it reaches the firm-ball stage (120°C/248°F). This should take 15–20 minutes. The mixture scorches easily so stir once or twice to scrape from the bottom of the pan and prevent it from sticking.

4   Remove from the heat. Add the anise extract, if using, and the colouring paste.

5   Quickly pour the mixture, without scraping, into the prepared tin. Cool for several hours or until firm.

6   Use the foil to lift the liquorice from the tin on to a chopping board. Remove the foil.

7   Using a buttered sharp knife, cut the mixture into 1cm/½ wide strips.

8   Serve immediately, or wrap individually in waxed paper or line a pretty tin or box with paper and place them inside it. Store for up to 1 month.

makes: about 20 sticks

125g/4¼oz butter, plus extra for greasing

400g/14oz/2 cups caster (superfine) sugar

400g/14oz sweetened condensed milk

250ml/8fl oz/1 cup golden (light corn) syrup

0.75ml/⅛ tsp salt

5ml/1 tsp anise extract (optional, for red liquorice sticks)

2.5ml/½ tsp black or red colouring paste

makes: about 24 drops

butter, for greasing

200g/7oz/1 cup caster (superfine) sugar

100g/3¾oz golden (light corn) syrup

100g/3¾oz black treacle (molasses)

100ml/3½fl oz/scant ½ cup water

2.5ml/½ tsp cream of tartar

3 star anise

60ml/4 tbsp liquid fruit pectin or
15g/½oz powdered fruit pectin

2.5ml/½ tsp salt

5ml/1 tsp anise extract

sea salt, to sprinkle on top

Liquorice star anise drops

These little liquorice drops are intensified by the addition of two types of anise: the oil from the anise seed and the seeds and seed-pod of the star anise. The added salt is inspired by Danish salt liquorice, although this version contains less salt than those as it can be a bit overpowering.

1 Grease a baking sheet and line with baking parchment, ensuring it is as smooth as possible.

2 Combine the sugar, syrup, black treacle, water and cream of tartar in a heavy pan. Stir over a low heat to dissolve the sugar. Add the star anise and boil until it reaches hard-ball stage (130°C/266°F).

3 In a separate bowl, combine the pectin (add 60ml/4 tbsp water if using powdered pectin) and salt.

4 Pour the pectin into the syrup and stir.

5 Continue to stir. Bring to the boil and boil until the syrup reaches the firm-ball stage (120°C/248°F). Immediately remove from the heat.

6 Stir in the anise extract. Remove and discard the star anise.

7 Pour drops of the the syrup on to the baking parchment-lined sheet and sprinkle with sea salt. Allow them to set for about 4 hours.

8 Serve immediately or store in an airtight container for up to 3 weeks.

CHOCOLATES AND CHOCOLATE CONFECTIONS

Think Valentine's Day. Think Easter. Think
Christmas. Think chocolate. What better way to
celebrate these holidays than with a selection of
home-made truffles and chocolate confections?
Ganache-filled truffles are simple to make and
lend themselves to flavourful partnerings. Even
easier is a nutty bark that can be broken into
bitesize bits. Tempered properly, these candies
will look like tiny jewels glistening with a dark and
flavourful, professional-looking glaze.

Smooth, sleek and sublime

Some home-made chocolates and chocolate confections can be made simply and beautifully without much fuss, while others can be laboured over with painstaking precision. Start by tasting a variety of chocolates to learn which type you like best. Most are labelled with a percentage, for example, 70 per cent dark (bittersweet) chocolate or 40 per cent milk chocolate. This is a way of letting the consumer know what percentage of pure cocoa bean is in the chocolate. The higher the number, the fewer other ingredients have been added. All of the recipes in this chapter include a recommendation for the percentage of chocolate to use.

Chocolate truffles are one of the easiest and most delicious types of confections to make. The base of truffles is a ganache, which is a mixture of melted chocolate and cream. The cream can be infused with spices, flowers, herbs, nuts, teas and coffees, adding variation and character.

The ganache, once set, can be rolled into balls and dusted in cocoa powder; no chocolate tempering is needed. However, if you have the time, enrobing the balls of ganache in thin layers of tempered chocolate adds texture and a beautiful finish. Squares of the ganache can also be hand-dipped into tempered chocolate.

Moulded chocolates are made by coating moulds with tempered chocolate and filling them with a range of centres, such as caramel, and topping with more chocolate. You can further embellish them by decorating the inside of the moulds with gold leaf or drizzling with a different coloured chocolate.

Chocolate barks, cups and coins are straightforward to make, involving only some melted chocolate that may be mixed with other ingredients, then spread out or formed into cups or drops.

Chocolate confections are always popular and can be eaten as snacks, desserts or given as gifts. Mini Chocolate Brownies are especially popular – or, for something a bit different, you could try making a version of the famous chocolate- and coconut-covered Australian cakes called Lamingtons.

Dark chocolate truffles

Smooth, creamy and intensely chocolatey, these classic truffles are a really decadent, grown-up treat. Use the best-quality chocolate you can, as this is what will really lend the truffles an extra-special edge. They are perfect for gifts, and look very attractive piled up in a box or tin or served in a glass bowl.

makes: about 50

120ml/4fl oz/½ cup double (heavy) cream

100g/3¾oz golden (light corn) syrup

1 vanilla pod (bean), split in half

350g/12oz dark (bittersweet) chocolate (66–70% cocoa solids), chopped

50g/2oz/4 tbsp unsalted butter, softened

unsweetened cocoa powder, for rolling

Cook's Tip

In this recipe the truffles are made into rough, rustic balls, but if you prefer you could roll them into neater, more perfect shapes.

1 Stir the cream and golden syrup together in a heavy pan, then scrape the vanilla seeds out of the pod and add to the pan along with the pod.

2 Heat over a low heat and bring to just below the boil (a foamy layer of cream should just be starting to form).

3 Remove from the heat, transfer to a bowl and cover with clear film (plastic wrap). Chill overnight.

4 Butter a 20cm/8in square baking tin (pan) and line with clear film (plastic wrap).

5 Place the chocolate in a medium stainless steel bowl and set over a barely simmering pan of water. Using a chocolate thermometer, heat to just below 46°C/115°F, then remove from the heat.

6 Meanwhile, place the bowl of cream golden syrup over a pan of simmering water and heat to just below 46°C/115°F.

7 Pour the melted chocolate and the cream into a blender and blend until it is thick and creamy. Alternatively, pour the liquids into a measuring jug (cup) and blend with an immersion blender.

8 Add the very soft butter, bit by bit, blending well between each addition so it is completely incorporated.

9 Pour the ganache into the prepared baking tin and smooth the surface with an offset spatula. Allow it to cool for a few hours until it has set. You can then place it into the refrigerator until you are ready to form the truffles.

10 To form the truffles, turn the ganache block out on to a marble or other cold, hard surface. Remove the clear film.

11 Dip a clean sharp knife in hot water, wipe it dry, then slice the ganache into 2cm/¾in squares.

12 Dust your palms and fingers with cocoa powder and roll the squares into rustic balls. Roll these in more cocoa powder.

13 Serve immediately, or place the truffles in a bag or container with extra cocoa powder (to prevent them from sticking together) and store in the refrigerator. Remove from the refrigerator at least 30 minutes before serving, as chocolate should be eaten at room temperature.

Grand Marnier chocolate truffles

makes: about 50

120ml/4fl oz/½ cup double (heavy) cream

100g/3¾oz golden (light corn) syrup

1 vanilla pod (bean), split in half

350g/12oz dark (bittersweet) chocolate (66–70% cocoa solids), chopped

50g/2oz/4 tbsp unsalted butter, softened

10ml/2 tsp Grand Marnier

100g/3¾oz candied orange peel, chopped and tossed in caster (superfine) sugar

Cook's Tip
Made with tropical oranges, the brandy pairs especially well with a fruity chocolate, such as Valrhona's 64% single estate type from Madagascar.

These adult treats contain the classic combination of Grand Marnier and dark chocolate. Finishing the truffles by rolling them in bits of candied orange peel adds both texture and additional flavour, as well as making them even prettier.

1 Stir the cream and golden syrup together in a heavy pan, then scrape the vanilla seeds out of the pod and add to the pan along with the pod.

2 Heat over a low heat and bring to just below the boil (a foamy layer of cream should just be starting to form).

3 Remove from the heat, transfer to a bowl and cover with clear film (plastic wrap). Chill overnight.

4 Butter a 20cm/8in square baking tin (pan) and line with clear film (plastic wrap).

5 Place the chocolate in a medium stainless steel bowl and set over a barely simmering pan of water. Using a chocolate thermometer, heat to just below 46°C/115°F, then remove from the heat.

6 Meanwhile, place the bowl of cream and golden syrup over a pan of simmering water and heat to just below 46°C/115°F.

7 Pour the melted chocolate and the heated cream into a blender and blend until it is thick and creamy. Alternatively, you can pour the liquids into a measuring jug (cup) and blend with an immersion blender.

8 Add the very soft butter, bit by bit, blending well between each addition so it is completely incorporated. Add the Grand Marnier and blend.

9 Pour the ganache into the prepared tin and smooth the surface with an offset spatula. Allow it to cool for a few hours until it has set. You can then place it into the refrigerator until you are ready to form the truffles.

10 To form the truffles, turn the ganache block out on to a marble or other cold, hard surface. Remove the clear film.

11 Dip a clean sharp knife in hot water, wipe it dry, then slice the ganache into 2cm/¾in squares.

12 Dust your palms and fingers with cocoa powder and roll the squares into balls. Roll these in the chopped candied peel.

13 Serve immediately, or place the truffles in a bag or container and store in the refrigerator. This can cause the sugar on the candied peel to melt, so you will need to toss them in caster sugar again. Remove from the refrigerator at least 30 minutes before serving, as chocolate should be eaten at room temperature.

Champagne truffles

makes: about 50

250g/9oz dark (bittersweet) chocolate (70% cocoa solids), chopped

200g/7oz milk chocolate (40% cocoa solids), chopped

150ml/¼ pint/⅔ cup double (heavy) cream

50g/2oz unsalted butter

100ml/3½fl oz/scant ½ cup champagne or other sparkling wine

15ml/1 tbsp brandy

700g/1lb 10oz dark chocolate (70% cocoa solids), tempered (*see* page 17)

icing (confectioners') sugar for rolling

edible gold dust (optional)

A version of this traditional classic is made by almost every good chocolatier. You could make them with any sparkling wine you like, such as prosecco or cava. Rosé champagne makes an especially delicious truffle. Here gold dust has been used, but you could also finish them with an extra roll in icing sugar.

1 Butter a 20cm/8in square baking tin (pan) and line with clear film (plastic wrap). Line a baking tray with baking parchment.

2 Put the dark and milk chocolate in a heatproof bowl and set aside.

3 Put the cream and butter in a small, heavy pan and heat to just under a boil over a moderate heat. Swirl the cream around every so often so that it does not burn around the edges of the pan.

4 Pour the heated cream over the chopped chocolate and leave it to sit for about a minute before adding the champagne and brandy.

5 Whisk by hand until all the chocolate is melted and you have a smooth ganache. Alternatively, use a hand-held immersion blender or blend the cream and chocolate in a food processor.

6 Pour the mixture into the prepared tin. Leave until the mixture begins to firm up.

7 To form the truffles, scrape the ganache up into a piping (pastry) bag fitted with a 1cm/½in plain nozzle. Pipe out even little blobs on to the parchment-lined baking tray.

8 Place in the refrigerator for about 20 minutes or until firm.

9 Dust your palms and fingers with icing sugar and roll the ganache blobs into balls. Return to the refrigerator for 10 minutes, until firm.

10 At this point you will need the tempered chocolate. Have ready a cooling rack and another baking sheet lined with parchment paper. Using a dipping fork, dunk each ball of ganache into the tempered dark chocolate and place on a cooling rack.

11 Roll the truffles in the gold dust, if using, or dip a clean, dry pastry brush into the pot of gold dust, then carefully hold it over the truffles. With the other hand, tap the handle of the brush. This will release the dust and allow it to fall freely and evenly over the truffles. Leave to set for about 30 minutes.

12 Serve immediately or store the champagne truffles in the refrigerator in an airtight container, spaced apart. Remove from the refrigerator at least 30 minutes before serving, as chocolate should be eaten at room temperature.

White chocolate espresso truffles

makes: about 50

250ml/8fl oz/1 cup double (heavy) cream

50g/2oz whole espresso beans

400g/14fl oz/1⅔ cups white chocolate, chopped

15ml/1 tbsp brandy

300g/11oz dark (bittersweet) chocolate (70% cocoa solids), tempered (*see* page 17)

550g/1lb 5oz white chocolate, tempered (*see* page 17)

10g/¼oz espresso beans, very finely ground (optional)

The combination of white and dark chocolate and silky coffee-flavoured truffle is absolutely delicious, and is especially irresistible if you are a coffee-lover. The dark chocolate will show through the final white chocolate layer of the truffle, but that is intentional, and is enhanced by the sprinkling of ground espresso beans. These are perfect after a special meal.

1 Line the base of a shallow baking tray with baking parchment.

2 Place the cream and espresso beans in a small pan over a moderate heat and bring to just under a boil. Allow the beans to steep for about 10 minutes, then heat the mixture to just under the boil again.

3 Place the chopped white chocolate in a bowl and, holding a fine-mesh sieve (strainer) above it to catch the espresso beans, pour in the hot cream.

4 Add the brandy and leave to cool. When the mixture is cool and the chocolate looks melted, whisk to form a smooth, creamy ganache. Take care not to overmix it as the white chocolate can seize up.

5 Leave the ganache for about 15 minutes to begin to firm up.

6 To form the truffles, scrape or pour the ganache up into a piping (pastry) bag fitted with a 5mm/¼in plain nozzle. If the ganache is still too soft, it will run right out of the pastry bag, so fill the bag over a clean bowl or jug (pitcher) to catch any drips.

7 Pipe out even little blobs on to the parchment-lined baking tray, then chill in the refrigerator for about 20 minutes or until the blobs are firm.

8 At this point you will need the tempered dark chocolate. Have ready a cooling rack and another baking tray lined with baking parchment.

9 Dip each ball of ganache into the tempered dark chocolate with a dipping fork and place on the cooling rack to set. If you don't have a dipping fork and have relatively cold hands, you can also dip the chocolates by hand, wearing latex gloves.

10 Using a clean dipping fork, dip each truffle into the tempered white chocolate. Place on the baking tray and leave for about 15 minutes, until set.

11 Sprinkle each truffle with a few tiny granules of ground espresso beans and serve immediately, or store in a container, spaced apart, in the refrigerator. Remove 30 minutes before serving, as chocolate should be eaten at room temperature.

Chocolate lips and hearts

makes: about 25

300g/11oz/1½ cups caster (superfine) sugar

50ml/2fl oz/¼ cup water

1 vanilla pod (bean), scraped

175ml/6fl oz/¾ cup double (heavy) cream

34ml/3 tbsp golden (light corn) syrup

90g/3½oz/7 tbsp unsalted butter, softened

a pinch salt

edible gold leaf (optional)

white or milk chocolate, tempered (*see* page 17), for drizzling, (optional)

500g/1¼lb dark (bittersweet) chocolate (64% cocoa solids or higher), tempered (*see* page 17)

Cook's Tip

Chocolate moulds can be found at cake decorating and speciality cooking stores. The thin plastic ones are fine for one or two uses, but if you plan on doing a lot of moulded chocolate-making, it is worth investing in a good, thick mould. Many different shapes are available, so choose ones that are appropriate for the occasion.

Lips and hearts are appropriate shapes for these rich, intense chocolates, which are perfect for a romantic dinner or Valentine's gift. They are quite fiddly to make – the trick is to make the chocolate shell just thick enough to contain the caramel, as a too-thick shell ruins the delicacy of the truffle.

1 Put the sugar and water into a large, heavy pan and heat over a medium heat, stirring, until the sugar is dissolved. Add the scraped vanilla seeds and the pod.

2 Continue to cook until the sugar syrup is a dark caramel colour, but don't let it burn. As soon as you see the first wisp of smoke it's done. Remove from the heat.

3 Meanwhile, pour the cream and golden syrup into a small pan and bring to the boil.

4 When the caramel is ready, slowly pour the cream mixture into it, taking great care that you don't burn your hand.

5 Whisk to release more of the steam and dissipate the bubbles. Stir in the butter and remove the vanilla pod.

6 Insert a sugar thermometer and let the caramel cool to 27°C/80°F. This can take a couple of hours. When it has cooled, pour it into a nozzled bottle and set aside.

7 If you want to decorate the outside of the chocolates (as shown in the photos), place pieces of gold leaf inside the heart moulds. Drizzle tempered white chocolate into the other moulds. Leave to set a little, then scrape away any excess chocolate.

8 Coat the moulds with most of the tempered dark chocolate. Hold the mould at an angle over a bowl so that the excess chocolate runs down, coating the inside of the mould and allowing any excess chocolate to drizzle out into the bowl.

9 Tap on a work surface to release any bubbles. Lay the mould upside down on a piece of baking parchment. After a few minutes check to see if the chocolate has begun to set on the sides.

10 Using a large palette knife or the back of a knife, scrape away any excess chocolate from the plastic surrounding moulds.

11 Return to the baking parchment and allow the chocolate to set fully before adding the filling. This will take about 1 hour.

12 Fill the moulds with the caramel, using a squirt bottle. Tap on a surface to release any bubbles. Leave to sit, uncovered, overnight.

13 Temper the remaining dark chocolate and spoon over the set caramel filling. Scrape any extra chocolate off the top and leave to set for 1–1½ hours.

14 Invert the moulds and tap lightly to release the chocolates. Serve.

Rose and violet creams

Old-fashioned and classic, chocolate creams made with sweet, delicate floral essences are becoming popular once again. You can make the dainty crystallized rose and violet petals, or they can be found at speciality supermarkets and delis.

1   Line a baking sheet with baking parchment or have a cooling rack ready.

2   Divide the fondant in half. Knead the violet syrup into one half of the fondant and knead the rose syrup into the other half. Roll them into two logs.

3   Cut each log into about 25 bitesize pieces and roll them into balls.

4   Dip each ball of fondant into tempered chocolate with a dipping fork, then place on the baking parchment or cooling rack.

5   Decorate the top of the rose creams with Crystalized Rose Petals and the top of the violet creams with violet petals. Leave to set for about 30 minutes.

6   Remove the rose and violet creams from the parchment or rack.

7   Serve immediately in mini paper cups or store in an airtight container, spaced apart, in the refrigerator. Remove 30 minutes before serving, as chocolate should be eaten at room temperature.

makes: about 50

300g/11oz fondant (*see* page 15)

2–3 drops rose syrup

2–3 drops violet syrup

400g/14oz dark (bittersweet) chocolate (at least 70% cocoa solids), tempered (*see* page 17)

Crystallized Rose Petals (*see* page 106) and candied violet petals (use the same method as for Crystallized Rose Petals, using violet petals)

makes: about 50

50ml/2fl oz/¼ cup cold water

200g/7oz/1 cup sugar

2.5m/½ tsp cream of tartar (optional)

225ml/8fl oz/scant 1 cup double
(heavy) cream

50g/2oz/4 tbsp unsalted butter,
plus extra for greasing

2.5ml/½ tsp sea salt, such as Hawaiian
pink salt, crushed

425g/15oz dark (bittersweet) chocolate
(70% cocoa solids), finely chopped

400g/14oz dark chocolate (70% cocoa
solids), for dipping

sea salt, for decoration

Salted caramel chocolates

These elegant chocolates consist of a dark caramel and sea salt ganache coated with a layer of yet more dark chocolate. Salt and caramel are a traditional combination, and it has become very fashionable to use it in confectionery.

1 Grease a 20cm/8in square cake tin (pan), then line with clear film (plastic wrap). Line a baking sheet with baking parchment.

2 Place the water in a heavy pan and cover with the sugar. Add the cream of tartar, if using. Heat gently to dissolve, stirring often.

3 Once the sugar has dissolved, turn the heat up to high and bring to the boil. Boil until the syrup caramelizes. It can be as light or as dark as you like; but do not burn it.

4 Slowly and carefully add the cream (it will spatter so use caution and wear oven gloves). Use a whisk to incorporate it fully.

5 Add the butter and salt and whisk until smooth. Put the chopped dark chocolate in a large, heatproof bowl.

6 With a whisk, combine the caramel and chocolate to form a smooth ganache.

7 Pour into the lined cake tin and smooth the top with an offset spatula. Leave to set for a couple of hours, then place in the refrigerator and chill for about 30 minutes.

8 Turn the ganache out on to a marble or other cold surface. Remove the clear film. Dip a knife in hot water, wipe it dry and use it to slice the block into 2cm/¾in squares.

9 Return to the refrigerator to chill for a further 30 minutes. Meanwhile, temper the remaining dark chocolate (see page 17).

10 Dip the chilled squares in the melted chocolate and transfer them to the prepared baking sheet. Sprinkle with sea salt. Leave to set for about 30 minutes.

11 Serve as they are or in individual paper or foil cups. Store in an airtight container, spaced apart, in the refrigerator.

White and dark chocolate bark

Chocolate barks are essentially sophisticated chocolate bars: the best way to enjoy a good-quality chocolate with a little extra embellishment. This recipe is very easy to make and takes hardly any time at all to prepare. The addition of crunchy sea salt is reminiscent of chocolate-covered pretzels.

1 Line a baking tray with baking parchment.
2 Place the chopped white chocolate in a heatproof bowl positioned over a pan of barely simmering water. Do not let the water touch the bottom of the bowl or the chocolate will burn. Stir occasionally to assist the melting.
3 Pour two-thirds of the white chocolate into the prepared baking tray.
4 Sprinkle with salt, then sprinkle with the chopped dark chocolate.
5 Immediately pour the remaining white chocolate over the top.

6 Spread the chocolate smooth with an offset spatula. Leave for 12–15 minutes, until set.
7 Slide the baking parchment on to a worktop. Place a cutting board on top of it and invert the bark. Carefully peel off the baking parchment.
8 Cut the bark into irregular pieces with a sharp knife.
9 Serve immediately or store in an airtight container in the refrigerator. Remove 30 minutes before serving, as chocolate should be eaten at room temperature.

makes: about 550g/1lb 5oz

500g/1¼ lb white chocolate, finely chopped

50g/2oz dark (bittersweet) chocolate (70% cocoa solids), finely chopped

5ml/1 tsp flakey sea salt, such as Maldon

Cook's Tip
Bark makes a great gift. Simply break the sheet up into big pieces and wrap these in baking parchment or waxed paper to stop any cocoa butter seeping through, then finish them with wrapping paper and a ribbon.

Flaked almond bark

This is one of the easiest and most delicious chocolate treats you can make, and it is extremely versatile. This recipe is for a bark made with flaked almonds suspended in dark chocolate and topped with pistachios, but you could use whichever combination of chocolate type and nut you prefer.

1 Line a baking sheet with clear film (plastic wrap) and set aside. Heat the oven to 160°C/325°F/Gas 3.

2 Spread the nuts out on another baking sheet and place in the preheated oven until just toasted. This should take about 7 minutes. Watch them closely so they don't burn and become bitter.

3 Melt the dark chocolate in a heatproof bowl positioned over a pan of barely simmering water. Stir it occasionally to help it melt.

4 Add the almonds to the chocolate and stir to combine. Quickly scrape the mixture into the prepared baking sheet and smooth the surface with an offset spatula.

5 Tap the sheet on a surface a few times to release any air bubbles.

6 Scatter the chopped pistachio nuts on top. Leave to set for 12–15 minutes. You can also put it in the refrigerator for a few minutes to help it set.

7 Remove by lifting it up by the edges of the clear film. Gently lean the pistachio side against your fingertips and peel away the clear film with the other hand.

8 Cut the bark into irregular pieces with a sharp knife.

9 Serve immediately or store in an airtight container in the refrigerator. Remove 30 minutes before serving, as chocolate should be eaten at room temperature.

makes: about 450g/1lb

200g/7oz/scant 2 cups flaked (sliced) almonds

200g/7oz dark (bittersweet) chocolate (55–64% cocoa solids)

50g/2oz/½ cup chopped pistachio nuts

Cook's Tip

If you chill the chocolate to help it set, it may shatter slightly when you start to cut the pieces of bark. To prevent this, allow the chocolate to come to room temperature before cutting it.

Chocolate berry cups

These lovely little chocolate cases are so easy to make and look fantastically cute and sophisticated. Dark chocolate and delicious berries are the perfect way to end a meal. You could also fill the chocolate cups with whipped cream or home-made chocolate mousse, if you like.

makes: 6

300g/11oz dark (bittersweet) chocolate (64–70% cocoa solids), tempered (*see* page 17)

600g/1lb 6oz berries, such as raspberries, mulberries or blackberries

200ml/7fl oz/scant 1 cup double (heavy) cream (optional)

caster (superfine) sugar or vanilla sugar, to sprinkle on top (optional)

1   Lay six paper cupcake cases out on a baking sheet, then double them up for extra support.

2   Pour a little tempered chocolate into a cupcake case. Using a clean, dry pastry brush or small paint brush, paint the inside with a layer of chocolate. Repeat with the other cases.

3   Leave to set for about 2 minutes, then paint on another layer.

4   Allow to set completely. This could take up to 5 hours. Peel away the papers and prepare the filling.

5   If you are using the cream, whip it to soft peaks and put some in each case. Fill with berries. If the berries are too tart, sprinkle with sugar to taste.

6   Serve immediately. You can store the cases in an airtight container in the refrigerator for up to a week, but once you have filled them they need to be served within a few hours.

VARIATION: Mash up some berries with a little sugar and swirl them through the whipped cream. Top with more berries.

Chocolate coins with candied fruit

These chocolate coins are studded with little gems of cut candied fruits and make an infinitely more sophisticated and thoughtful present than store-bought ones. They are also a great way to use up any candied fruits left over after making a mincemeat or other festive desserts.

makes: about 24

butter, for greasing

50g/2oz candied fruit

200g/7oz dark (bittersweet) chocolate (64–70% cocoa solids), tempered (*see* page 17)

1 Smear little blobs of butter on a baking sheet, then line with baking parchment.

2 Slice the candied fruit into small, attractive pieces.

3 Put the tempered chocolate in a funnel with a catch or use a teaspoon to drop small rounds of chocolate on to the baking parchment.

4 Quickly decorate the tops with the slices of candied fruit. It may best to do this in batches, or enlist the help of a child to add the fruit.

5 Allow the chocolate to set completely for about an hour, then peel away from the paper and place on a pretty serving dish or into a tin (pan) lined with paper. You can also place these in individual paper cups.

6 Store in an airtight container in a cool place for up to a week. The candied fruit may bleed if they are refrigerated, so it is best to avoid doing this.

VARIATION: For children, use milk chocolate and top with sweets (candies).

Chocolate boats

Buttery sweetcrust pastry boats are the perfect vehicle for some rich, dark chocolate ganache. You can prepare the pastry shells in advance, then simply create the ganache at the last minute, making these easy and elegant petit fours for a special occasion. You will need boat moulds.

1 To make the pastry, cream the butter and sugar until light but not too fluffy.
2 Add the flour and salt and mix until just combined. Add the egg yolk and bring together into a ball. Wrap in clear film (plastic wrap) and press into a disc. Place in the refrigerator to chill for about 30 minutes.
3 When the dough is firm but not hard, remove it from the refrigerator. Lightly dust a work surface and the dough with flour.
4 Roll out the dough to about 3mm/⅛in thickness. The pastry boats need to be strong enough to stand on their own, but not so thick that they dominate the chocolate.
5 Cut teardrop shapes that are slightly larger than the boat moulds. Use a knife or offset spatula to gently lift them up off the counter and into the moulds. Press them into place and trim off any excess pastry.

6 Place the moulds on a baking sheet and chill for 15 minutes. Meanwhile, preheat the oven to 180°C/350°F/Gas 4.
7 Bake for about 7 minutes, until just golden on the edges and cooked through.
8 Leave to cool, then remove them from their moulds and transfer to a serving tray.
9 To make the filling, place the cream and golden syrup or glucose in a small pan and bring to the boil.
10 Put the chopped chocolate in a large, heatproof bowl and pour the hot cream over it. Stir every few minutes until the chocolate is melted.
11 Spoon the ganache into the pastry shells. Serve immediately or store in an airtight container in the refrigerator for up to 3 days. Allow to come to room temperature before serving.

makes: about 24

For the pastry

115g/4oz unsalted butter, softened

50g/2oz/¼ cup caster (superfine) sugar

175g/6oz/1½ cups plain (all-purpose) flour

a pinch salt

½ egg yolk

For the filling

60ml/4 tbsp double (heavy) cream

50ml/2fl oz/¼ cup golden (light corn) syrup or liquid glucose

175g/6oz dark (bittersweet) chocolate (64–70% cocoa solids), finely chopped

300g/11oz dark (bittersweet) chocolate (70% cocoa solids), chopped

125g/4¼oz/9 tbsp unsalted butter

3 eggs

175g/6oz light brown sugar

2.5ml/½ tsp sea salt

2.5ml/½ tsp vanilla extract

100g/3¾oz/scant 1 cup plain (all-purpose) flour

150g/5oz dark chocolate (55–64% cocoa solids), chopped into 1cm/½in pieces

Mini chocolate brownies

There are countless recipes for brownies and as many reasons why each particular recipe is favoured. This is a recipe for those who like a combination of cakey and moist, gooey texture. The pieces of chocolate that melt into it create pockets of pure chocolate flavour – heaven!

1 Preheat the oven to 160°C/325°F/Gas 3.

2 Butter a 20cm/8in square cake tin (pan) with baking parchment so that it comes up the sides of the tin.

3 Melt the chopped chocolate (70% cocoa solids) and butter in a heatproof bowl placed over a pan of barely simmering water, stirring every few minutes. When melted, remove and leave to cool slightly.

4 In a clean bowl, whisk the eggs, sugar, salt and vanilla until frothy and light.

5 Fold the melted chocolate into the egg mixture, then fold in flour and chocolate pieces. Transfer to the prepared cake tin.

6 Bake for exactly 27 minutes, so that the top is just set but the insides are still gooey. All ovens differ a little, but it is so important for the texture of the brownies not to let them overcook. If you think your oven is a little cool than give it another minute, but they will seem a little soft when they are done. Remember, they continue to set as they cool.

7 Remove from the oven and leave to cool in the tin. When they have cooled, remove from the tin and cut into squares. Serve immediately or store in an airtight container for up to 4 days.

makes: 20–30

125g/4¼oz/generous ½ cup butter, softened, plus extra for greasing

125g/4¼oz/scant ¾ cup caster (superfine) sugar

3 egg whites

100g/3¾oz/generous ¾ cup plain (all-purpose) flour, plus extra for dusting

25g/1oz/¼ cup unsweetened cocoa powder

Cook's Tip

If they go soft during storage, put the tuiles into an oven preheated to 180°C/350°F/Gas 4 for 3 minutes to dry out any moisture they may have absorbed from the air and re-crisp.

Chocolate tuiles

Light and crisp, these are the perfect accompaniment to ice cream or chocolate mousse. You can pipe them into shapes or bend them while they are hot, or leave them in long flat strips. You could also form them into the first letters of people's names to add a personal touch to a special dessert.

1 Grease a baking sheet and dust it with flour. Preheat the oven to 180°C/350°F/Gas 4.

2 Cream the soft butter and sugar until light and fluffy. Add the egg whites and incorporate fully.

3 Sift the flour and cocoa powder over the mixture and fold it in with a rubber spatula or metal spoon. Try not to overmix the batter or it will become tough.

4 Pour the mixture into a piping (pastry) bag and pipe into shapes or use moulds to create shapes. Bake in the oven for 6–8 minutes, until just golden.

5 Remove from the oven. If you want to shape them at this stage, very quickly wrap them around a rolling pin or the handle of a wooden spoon, then slide them off on to a wire rack to cool. They start to set as soon as you remove them from the oven, so you need to do this quickly.

6 Leave to cool, then serve. Store in an airtight container for up to 3 days.

VARIATION: You can make plain versions of these by simply substituting the cocoa with more plain (all-purpose) flour, or add orange or lemon zest for added flavour.

Mini lamingtons

These delicious cakes are a favourite treat in Australia, and are quickly gaining in popularity in the UK. The test of a true lamington is in the texture of the sponge. It must be moist and fluffy, but incredibly airy. The chocolate glaze and crumbly coconut coating brings it all together to form a light, sweet treat.

1 Preheat the oven to 160°C/325°F/Gas 3. Butter a 20 x 30cm/8 x 12in cake tin (pan) and line with baking parchment.

2 To make the cake, beat the eggs with an electric mixer until they begin to froth, then add the sugar. Beat until light and fluffy.

3 Sift the flour and cornflour over the eggs and fold together with a rubber spatula or metal spoon.

4 Combine the melted butter and hot water in a measuring jug (cup) and fold into the cake mixture.

5 Pour the mixture into the prepared tin and bake for about 25–30 minutes, until just set and coming away from the edge of the tin slightly.

6 Remove from the oven and leave to cool for about 10 minutes before turning the cake out on to a cooling rack.

7 When it is completely cooled, cut the cake into 12–15 pieces.

8 Put the coconut in a wide, shallow dish and set aside.

9 To make the icing, put all of the ingredients into a heatproof bowl placed over a pan of simmering water. Using a whisk, stir constantly to make an emulsified icing. Turn off the heat, but leave the bowl over the hot water.

10 With a dipping fork, dip each piece of cake into the icing. Wipe the bottom of the cake along the edge of the bowl to remove excess icing. Gently place the dipped cake into the coconut and turn to coat.

11 Place the lamingtons on a clean wire rack and leave to set for about 15 minutes. Serve immediately, or store in an airtight container for up to 3 days.

makes: 12–15

For the cake:

butter, for greasing

3 eggs

100g/3½oz/generous ½ cup caster (superfine) sugar

100g/3½oz/generous ¾ cup self-raising (self-rising) flour

35g/1½oz/scant ½ cup cornflour (cornstarch)

15g/½oz/1 tbsp butter, melted

45ml/3 tbsp hot water

300g/11oz/scant 3 cups desiccated (dry unsweetened) coconut

For the icing:

15g/½oz/1 tbsp butter

375g/13oz/3¼ cups icing (confectioners') sugar, sifted

150g/5oz dark (bittersweet) chocolate (55% cocoa solids), chopped

90ml/6 tbsp milk

Nutritional notes

Pear drops Per total amount: Energy 1841kcal/7860kJ; Protein 2.4g; Carbohydrate 488.1g, of which sugars 488.1g; Fat 0.2g, of which saturates 0g; Cholesterol 0mg; Calcium 251mg; Fibre 0g; Sodium 31mg.

Raspberry lollipops Per total amount: Energy 1651kcal/7051kJ; Protein 6.2g; Carbohydrate 431.8g, of which sugars 431.8g; Fat 0.9g, of which saturates 0.3g; Cholesterol 0mg; Calcium 287mg; Fibre 7.5g; Sodium 33mg.

Jewelled lollipops Per total amount: Energy 157kcal/668kJ; Protein 0.6g; Carbohydrate 38.4g, of which sugars 37.8g; Fat 1.2g, of which saturates 0.2g; Cholesterol 0mg; Calcium 22mg; Fibre 0.2g; Sodium 16mg.

Aniseed twists Per total amount: Energy 1894kcal/8079kJ; Protein 2g; Carbohydrate 502.7g, of which sugars 458.2g; Fat 0g, of which saturates 0g; Cholesterol 0mg; Calcium 220mg; Fibre 0g; Sodium 17mg.

Lemon drops Per total amount: Energy 2412kcal/10289kJ; Protein 3g; Carbohydrate 639.7g, of which sugars 633g; Fat 0g, of which saturates 0g; Cholesterol 0mg; Calcium 319mg; Fibre 0g; Sodium 59mg.

Rhubarb and custards Per total amount: Energy 2015kcal/ 8595kJ; Protein 2.5g; Carbohydrate 534.4g, of which sugars 534.4g; Fat 0g, of which saturates 0g; Cholesterol 0mg; Calcium 269mg; Fibre 0g; Sodium 71mg.

Peppermint humbugs Per total amount: Energy 1621kcal/6914kJ; Protein 2g; Carbohydrate 429.9g, of which sugars 429.9g; Fat 0g, of which saturates 0g; Cholesterol 0mg; Calcium 216mg; Fibre 0g; Sodium 65mg.

Rose water Edinburgh rock Per total amount: Energy 1821kcal/7768kJ; Protein 2.3g; Carbohydrate 483g, of which sugars 476.3g; Fat 0g, of which saturates 0g; Cholesterol 0mg; Calcium 240mg; Fibre 0g; Sodium 50mg.

Salt-water taffy Per total amount: Energy 1502kcal/6378kJ; Protein 1.2g; Carbohydrate 349.9g, of which sugars 269.3g; Fat 20.5g, of which saturates 13.5g; Cholesterol 58mg; Calcium 124mg; Fibre 0g; Sodium 1022mg.

Lemon cream dreams Per portion: Energy 62kcal/262kJ; Protein 0.2g; Carbohydrate 15g, of which sugars 15g; Fat 0.5g, of which saturates 0.1g; Cholesterol 0mg; Calcium 10mg; Fibre 0.1g; Sodium 10mg.

Fruit sherbet Per total amount: Energy 1970kcal/8405kJ; Protein 2.5g; Carbohydrate 522.5g, of which sugars 522.5g; Fat 0g, of which saturates 0g; Cholesterol 0mg; Calcium 265mg; Fibre 0g; Sodium 30mg.

Nutty chocolate toffee Per total amount: Energy 4254kcal/17814kJ; Protein 60.8g; Carbohydrate 498g, of which sugars 477.5g; Fat 237.9g, of which saturates 109.3g; Cholesterol 301mg; Calcium 456mg; Fibre 12.4g; Sodium 993mg.

Pecan toffees Per total amount: Energy 2536kcal/10698kJ; Protein 13.6g; Carbohydrate 451.4g, of which sugars 449.5g; Fat 87.6g, of which saturates 7.1g; Cholesterol 0mg; Calcium 302mg; Fibre 5.9g; Sodium 27mg.

Cinder toffee Per total amount: Energy 931kcal/3973kJ; Protein 1.2g; Carbohydrate 247g, of which sugars 247g; Fat 0g, of which saturates 0g; Cholesterol 0mg; Calcium 123mg; Fibre 0g; Sodium 54mg.

Honeycomb toffee Per total amount: Energy 3350kcal/14147kJ; Protein 4.4g; Carbohydrate 643.2g, of which sugars 643.2g; Fat 102.1g, of which saturates 67.5g; Cholesterol 288mg; Calcium 783mg; Fibre 0g; Sodium 1598mg.

Bonfire toffee Per total amount: Energy 2386kcal/10037kJ; Protein 4.5g; Carbohydrate 386.3g, of which sugars 386.3g; Fat 102.1g, of which saturates 67.5g; Cholesterol 288mg; Calcium 1263mg; Fibre 0g; Sodium 1167mg.

Burnt caramel shards Per total amount: Energy 1919kcal/8074kJ; Protein 2g; Carbohydrate 313.5g, of which sugars 313.5g; Fat 81.7g, of which saturates 54g; Cholesterol 230mg; Calcium 174mg; Fibre 0g; Sodium 768mg.

Salted caramels Per total amount: Energy 4746kcal/19870kJ; Protein 10.6g; Carbohydrate 607.9g, of which sugars 607.9g; Fat 294.8g, of which saturates 170.1g; Cholesterol 735mg; Calcium 505mg; Fibre 0g; Sodium 1286mg.

Fresh coconut and cardamom caramels Per total amount: Energy 4419kcal/18575kJ; Protein 11.4g; Carbohydrate 691.4g, of which sugars 691.4g; Fat 208.2g, of which saturates 134.6g; Cholesterol 408mg; Calcium 454mg; Fibre 10.3g; Sodium 1049mg.

Caramel-pecan chews Per portion: Energy 113kcal/473kJ; Protein 0.4g; Carbohydrate 12.8g, of which sugars 12.8g; Fat 7.6g, of which saturates 3.7g; Cholesterol 15mg; Calcium 12mg; Fibre 0.1g; Sodium 27mg.

Caramel apples Per portion: Energy 366kcal/1534kJ; Protein 0.8g; Carbohydrate 46.9g, of which sugars 46.9g; Fat 21.9g, of which saturates 13.4g; Cholesterol 57mg; Calcium 33mg; Fibre 1.1g; Sodium 160mg.

Butterscotch Per total amount: Energy 2987kcal/12529kJ; Protein 5g; Carbohydrate 422.1g, of which sugars 422.1g; Fat 162.3g, of which saturates 99g; Cholesterol 425mg; Calcium 302mg; Fibre 0g; Sodium 830mg.

Honey-sesame crunch Per total amount: Energy 1878kcal/7850kJ; Protein 37.3g; Carbohydrate 182.7g, of which sugars 181.7g; Fat 116g, of which saturates 16.6g; Cholesterol 0mg; Calcium 1398mg; Fibre 15.8g; Sodium 57mg.

Peanut brittle Per total amount: Energy 2626kcal/11011kJ; Protein 65.3g; Carbohydrate 305g, of which sugars 289.2g; Fat 135.4g, of which saturates 34g; Cholesterol 58mg; Calcium 276mg; Fibre 15.5g; Sodium 514mg.

Hazelnut praline Per total amount: Energy 2876kcal/12094kJ; Protein 30.2g; Carbohydrate 430g, of which sugars 426g; Fat 127g, of which saturates 9.4g; Cholesterol 0mg; Calcium 492mg; Fibre 13g; Sodium 36mg.

Caramel-buttered popcorn Per total amount: Energy 1440kcal/6054kJ; Protein 6.3g; Carbohydrate 232.8g, of which sugars 186.3g; Fat 60g, of which saturates 6g; Cholesterol 54mg; Calcium 18mg; Fibre 0g; Sodium 168mg.

Peanut popcorn Per total amount: Energy 3570kcal/14934kJ; Protein 73.5g; Carbohydrate 380.4g, of which sugars 294.9g; Fat 205g, of which saturates 29.5g; Cholesterol 81mg; Calcium 177mg; Fibre 15.5g; Sodium 257mg.

Vanilla fudge Per total amount: Energy 4665kcal/19743kJ; Protein 14.7g; Carbohydrate 954.9g, of which sugars 954.9g; Fat 113.8g, of which saturates 74.7g; Cholesterol 330mg; Calcium 841mg; Fibre 0g; Sodium 1157mg.

Old-fashioned chocolate fudge Per total amount: Energy 5707kcal/24098kJ; Protein 28.8g; Carbohydrate 1074.8g, of which sugars 1056.3g; Fat 173.2g, of which saturates 105.6g; Cholesterol 239mg; Calcium 856mg; Fibre 0g; Sodium 787mg.

Almond milk fudge Per total amount: Energy 6842kcal/28342kJ; Protein 115.5g; Carbohydrate 230.9g, of which sugars 217.4g; Fat 641.5g, of which saturates 235.6g; Cholesterol 915mg; Calcium 1560mg; Fibre 37g; Sodium 1128mg.

Espresso-macadamia fudge Per total amount: Energy 9614kcal/40330kJ; Protein 133.6g; Carbohydrate 1257.1g, of which sugars 1223.5g; Fat 501.6g, of which saturates 226.8g; Cholesterol 675mg; Calcium 1665mg; Fibre 22.3g; Sodium 1851mg.

Candied clementine fudge Per total amount: Energy 7450kcal/31305kJ; Protein 38.9g; Carbohydrate 1132.5g, of which sugars 1132.5g; Fat 355.4g, of which saturates 209.5g; Cholesterol 620mg; Calcium 1746mg; Fibre 7.2g; Sodium 1860mg.

Peanut butter fudge Per total amount: Energy 8274kcal/34696kJ; Protein 96.6g; Carbohydrate 1091g, of which sugars 1068g; Fat 434.7g, of which saturates 185.1g; Cholesterol 572mg; Calcium 791mg; Fibre 19.8g; Sodium 2705mg.

Yogurt pecan fudge Per total amount: Energy 3267kcal/13719kJ; Protein 27.7g; Carbohydrate 467.3g, of which sugars 465g; Fat 156.4g, of which saturates 42.1g; Cholesterol 141mg; Calcium 748mg; Fibre 7g; Sodium 743mg.

Rocky road fudge Per total amount: Energy 11632kcal/49052kJ; Protein 73.2g; Carbohydrate 2067.8g, of which sugars 2006g; Fat 397.8g, of which saturates 215.5g; Cholesterol 478mg; Calcium 1695mg; Fibre 3.2g; Sodium 1611mg.

Vanilla tablet Per total amount: Energy 5232kcal/22142kJ; Protein 26.9g; Carbohydrate 1058.7g, of which sugars 1058.7g; Fat 128.2g, of which saturates 83.7g; Cholesterol 381mg; Calcium 1248mg; Fibre 0g; Sodium 1354mg.

Fig tablet Per total amount: Energy 4223kcal/17946kJ; Protein 12.9g; Carbohydrate 996.3g, of which sugars 996.3g; Fat 48.2g, of which saturates 30.6g; Cholesterol 136mg; Calcium 887mg; Fibre 6.9g; Sodium 569mg.

Sour cherry panforte Per total amount: Energy 4078kcal/17190kJ; Protein 71g; Carbohydrate 665.1g, of which sugars 559.6g; Fat 144.7g, of which saturates 12.2g; Cholesterol 0mg; Calcium 1228mg; Fibre 34g; Sodium 886mg.

Coconut date rolls Per portion: Energy 63kcal/264kJ; Protein 0.7g; Carbohydrate 9.7g, of which sugars 9.7g; Fat 2.6g, of which saturates 2.2g; Cholesterol 0mg; Calcium 7mg; Fibre 1.1g; Sodium 3mg.

Coconut ice Per total amount: Energy 4682kcal/19746kJ; Protein 20.1g; Carbohydrate 816.1g, of which sugars 816.1g; Fat 171.4g, of which saturates 147.4g; Cholesterol 0mg; Calcium 548mg; Fibre 37.7g; Sodium 452mg.

Chocolate macaroons Per portion: Energy 93kcal/390kJ; Protein 0.9g; Carbohydrate 11.6g, of which sugars 11.3g; Fat 5.1g, of which saturates 3.9g; Cholesterol 1mg; Calcium 7mg; Fibre 0.8g; Sodium 9mg.

Vanilla bean marshmallows Per total amount: Energy 2224kcal/9481kJ; Protein 59g; Carbohydrate 529g, of which sugars 476.3g; Fat 0.3g, of which saturates 0.1g; Cholesterol 0mg; Calcium 250mg; Fibre 0.1g; Sodium 197mg.

Raspberry heart marshmallows Per total amount: Energy 2274kcal/9699kJ; Protein 61.8g; Carbohydrate 538.2g, of which sugars 485.5g; Fat 0.9g, of which saturates 0.3g; Cholesterol 0mg; Calcium 300mg; Fibre 5g; Sodium 203mg.

Two-tone marshmallow sticks Per total amount: Energy 2224kcal/9481kJ; Protein 59g; Carbohydrate 529g, of which sugars 476.3g; Fat 0.3g, of which saturates 0.1g; Cholesterol 0mg; Calcium 250mg; Fibre 0.1g; Sodium 197mg.

Almond meringue kisses Per total amount: Energy 1088kcal/4565kJ; Protein 27.4g; Carbohydrate 127.1g, of which sugars 124.4g; Fat 55.8g, of which saturates 4.7g; Cholesterol 0mg; Calcium 304mg; Fibre 7.4g; Sodium 143mg.

Strawberry meringue clouds Per total amount: Energy 1981kcal/8250kJ; Protein 13.1g; Carbohydrate 167.9g, of which sugars 167.9g; Fat 161.3g, of which saturates 90g; Cholesterol 390mg; Calcium 259mg; Fibre 2.4g; Sodium 249mg.

Melting chocolate meringues Per total amount: Energy 1001kcal/4228kJ; Protein 11g; Carbohydrate 185g, of which sugars 179.7g; Fat 29.2g, of which saturates 16.9g; Cholesterol 9mg; Calcium 102mg; Fibre 0g; Sodium 438mg.

Sea foam Per total amount: Energy 1628kcal/6942kJ; Protein 3.5g; Carbohydrate 430.1g, of which sugars 423.4g; Fat 0g, of which saturates 0g; Cholesterol 0mg; Calcium 242mg; Fibre 1.1g; Sodium 104mg.

Walnut and apricot divinity Per total amount: Energy 2273kcal/9620kJ; Protein 18.9g; Carbohydrate 461.2g, of which sugars 460.7g; Fat 51.8g, of which saturates 4.2g; Cholesterol 0mg; Calcium 330mg; Fibre 7.3g; Sodium 234mg.

Cherry divinity drops Per total amount: Energy 2483kcal/10586kJ; Protein 8.6g; Carbohydrate 652.4g, of which sugars 599g; Fat 0g, of which saturates 0g; Cholesterol 0mg; Calcium 337mg; Fibre 1.8g; Sodium 380mg.

Fresh nougat with candied fruit Per total amount: Energy 5644kcal/23755kJ; Protein 62.8g; Carbohydrate 870.1g, of which sugars 859.8g; Fat 233.4g, of which saturates 36.8g; Cholesterol 92mg; Calcium 1171mg; Fibre 36.4g; Sodium 1388mg.

Pistachio nougat Per total amount: Energy 4838kcal/20294kJ; Protein 103.3g; Carbohydrate 577.8g, of which sugars 554.5g; Fat 251.1g, of which saturates 21.1g; Cholesterol 0mg; Calcium 1293mg; Fibre 33.3g; Sodium 264mg.

Sugar mice Per portion: Energy 194kcal/826kJ; Protein 0.9g; Carbohydrate 45.3g, of which sugars 43.2g; Fat 2.3g, of which saturates 1.4g; Cholesterol 0mg; Calcium 31mg; Fibre 0.1g; Sodium 18mg.

Sugar Easter egg Per total amount: Energy 3956kcal/16879kJ; Protein 9.1g; Carbohydrate 1045g, of which sugars 1045g; Fat 0g, of which saturates 0g; Cholesterol 0mg; Calcium 532mg; Fibre 0g; Sodium 146mg.

Candied citrus peel Per total amount: Energy 2772kcal/11808kJ; Protein 3.6g; Carbohydrate 709.2g, of which sugars 709.2g; Fat 10.8g, of which saturates 0g; Cholesterol 0mg; Calcium 1560mg; Fibre 57.6g; Sodium 3360mg.

Candied stem ginger Per total amount: Energy 2723kcal/11612kJ; Protein 3.7g; Carbohydrate 721.7g, of which sugars 721.7g; Fat 0g, of which saturates 0g; Cholesterol 0mg; Calcium 433mg; Fibre 2.7g; Sodium 111mg.

Candied pineapple Per total amount: Energy 4186kcal/17866kJ; Protein 7.4g; Carbohydrate 1105.6g, of which sugars 1105.6g; Fat 1.2g, of which saturates 0g; Cholesterol 0mg; Calcium 638mg; Fibre 7.2g; Sodium 72mg.

Crystallized rose petals Per total amount: Energy 406kcal/1730kJ; Protein 3.4g; Carbohydrate 104.5g, of which sugars 104.5g; Fat 0g, of which saturates 0g; Cholesterol 0mg; Calcium 55mg; Fibre 0g; Sodium 67mg.

Turkish delight Per total amount: Energy 2971kcal/12672kJ; Protein 3.9g; Carbohydrate 786.5g, of which sugars 717.5g; Fat 0.5g, of which saturates 0.1g; Cholesterol 0mg; Calcium 358mg; Fibre 0.1g; Sodium 84mg.

Pineapple chews Per portion: Energy 61kcal/259kJ; Protein 0.2g; Carbohydrate 13.8g, of which sugars 13.8g; Fat 0.9g, of which saturates 0.6g; Cholesterol 2mg; Calcium 13mg; Fibre 0g; Sodium 9mg.

Ginger gumdrops Per total amount: Energy 2269kcal/9675kJ; Protein 19.8g; Carbohydrate 582.6g, of which sugars 536.6g; Fat 0.3g, of which saturates 0.1g; Cholesterol 0mg; Calcium 302mg; Fibre 1g; Sodium 80mg.

Two-tone jellies Per portion: Energy 70kcal/298kJ; Protein 0.2g; Carbohydrate 18.3g, of which sugars 18.3g; Fat 0g, of which saturates 0g; Cholesterol 0mg; Calcium 11mg; Fibre 0.2g; Sodium 7mg.

Blackberry paste Per portion: Energy 70kcal/297kJ; Protein 0.3g; Carbohydrate 18.2g, of which sugars 18.2g; Fat 0g, of which saturates 0g; Cholesterol 0mg; Calcium 17mg; Fibre 0.6g; Sodium 6mg.

Quince paste Per portion: Energy 86kcal/369kJ; Protein 0.2g; Carbohydrate 22.8g, of which sugars 22.8g; Fat 0g, of which saturates 0g; Cholesterol 0mg; Calcium 11mg; Fibre 0.3g; Sodium 2mg.

Baked pear crisps Per portion: Energy 85kcal/362kJ; Protein 0.1g; Carbohydrate 22.4g, of which sugars 22.4g; Fat 0g, of which saturates 0g; Cholesterol 0mg; Calcium 12mg; Fibre 0.3g; Sodium 2mg.

Simple almond paste Per total amount: Energy 2020kcal/8525kJ; Protein 26.5g; Carbohydrate 338g, of which sugars 338g; Fat 63.5g, of which saturates 6g; Cholesterol 0mg; Calcium 330mg; Fibre 9.5g; Sodium 100mg.

Boiled marzipan Per total amount: Energy 2424kcal/10230kJ; Protein 18.1g; Carbohydrate 405.6g, of which sugars 405.6g; Fat 76.2g, of which saturates 7.2g; Cholesterol 0mg; Calcium 396mg; Fibre 11.4g; Sodium 120mg.

Marzipan bumblebees Per portion: Energy 67kcal/281kJ; Protein 1g; Carbohydrate 10.2g, of which sugars 10.2g; Fat 2.5g, of which saturates 0.2g; Cholesterol 0mg; Calcium 12mg; Fibre 0.4g; Sodium 3mg.

Orange-almond morsels Per portion: Energy 56kcal/234kJ; Protein 0.6g; Carbohydrate 8.3g, of which sugars 8.1g; Fat 2.3g, of which saturates 0.8g; Cholesterol 0mg; Calcium 7mg; Fibre 0.2g; Sodium 2mg.

Espresso-hazelnut balls Per portion: Energy 52kcal/219kJ; Protein 1.2g; Carbohydrate 4.3g, of which sugars 4.2g; Fat 3.5g, of which saturates 0.3g; Cholesterol 2mg; Calcium 12mg; Fibre 0.4g; Sodium 1mg.

Mazipan stuffed hazelnuts Per portion: Energy 45kcal/186kJ; Protein 0.8g; Carbohydrate 3.6g, of which sugars 3.5g; Fat 3g, of which saturates 0.2g; Cholesterol 0mg; Calcium 9mg; Fibre 0.3g; Sodium 1mg

Stuffed dates Per portion: Energy 92kcal/388kJ; Protein 1.3g; Carbohydrate 15g, of which sugars 14.9g; Fat 2.8g, of which saturates 0.3g; Cholesterol 0mg; Calcium 15mg; Fibre 0.7g; Sodium 13mg.

Cherry-almond stars Per portion: Energy 30kcal/126kJ; Protein 0.7g; Carbohydrate 3.3g, of which sugars 3.2g; Fat 1.6g, of which saturates 0.1g; Cholesterol 0mg; Calcium 8mg; Fibre 0.2g; Sodium 2mg.

Liquorice shards Per total amount: Energy 1343kcal/5727kJ; Protein 2.5g; Carbohydrate 355.2g, of which sugars 355.2g; Fat 0g, of which saturates 0g; Cholesterol 0mg; Calcium 632mg; Fibre 0g; Sodium 1361mg.

Pontefract cakes Per total amount: Energy 1668kcal/7114kJ; Protein 3.1g; Carbohydrate 441.2g, of which sugars 441.2g; Fat 0g, of which saturates 0g; Cholesterol 0mg; Calcium 785mg; Fibre 0g; Sodium 1690mg.

Liquorice sticks Per portion: Energy 229kcal/965kJ; Protein 1.9g; Carbohydrate 41.9g, of which sugars 41.9g; Fat 7.1g, of which saturates 4.6g; Cholesterol 22mg; Calcium 73mg; Fibre 0g; Sodium 125mg.

Liquorice star anise drops Per portion: Energy 56kcal/239kJ; Protein 0.1g; Carbohydrate 14.8g, of which sugars 14.8g; Fat 0g, of which saturates 0g; Cholesterol 0mg; Calcium 26mg; Fibre 0g; Sodium 57mg.

Dark chocolate truffles Per portion: Energy 62kcal/256kJ; Protein 0.4g; Carbohydrate 3.6g, of which sugars 3.6g; Fat 5g, of which saturates 3.1g; Cholesterol 9mg; Calcium 4mg; Fibre 0.1g; Sodium 6mg.

Grand Marnier chocolate truffles Per portion: Energy 66kcal/277kJ; Protein 0.4g; Carbohydrate 7.4g, of which sugars 7g; Fat 4.2g, of which saturates 2.5g; Cholesterol 6mg; Calcium 7mg; Fibre 0.1g; Sodium 20mg.

Champagne truffles Per portion: Energy 144kcal/601kJ; Protein 1.3g; Carbohydrate 14.8g, of which sugars 13.7g; Fat 9.2g, of which saturates 5.4g; Cholesterol 9mg; Calcium 18mg; Fibre 0g; Sodium 16mg.

White chocolate espresso truffles Per portion: Energy 155kcal/647kJ; Protein 1.9g; Carbohydrate 15.1g, of which sugars 14.8g; Fat 10.3g, of which saturates 6g; Cholesterol 7mg; Calcium 56mg; Fibre 0g; Sodium 23mg.

Chocolate lips and hearts Per portion: Energy 83kcal/349kJ; Protein 0.2g; Carbohydrate 13.8g, of which sugars 13.8g; Fat 3.8g, of which saturates 2.1g; Cholesterol 9mg; Calcium 10mg; Fibre 0g; Sodium 7mg.

Rose and violet creams Per portion: Energy 66kcal/278kJ; Protein 0.5g; Carbohydrate 10.5g, of which sugars 9.9g; Fat 2.8g, of which saturates 1.6g; Cholesterol 1mg; Calcium 6mg; Fibre 0g; Sodium 2mg.

Salted caramel chocolates Per portion: Energy 130kcal/543kJ; Protein 0.9g; Carbohydrate 15g, of which sugars 14.1g; Fat 8.1g, of which saturates 4.7g; Cholesterol 10mg; Calcium 11mg; Fibre 0g; Sodium 11mg.

White and dark chocolate bark Per total amount: Energy 2908kcal/12159kJ; Protein 42.4g; Carbohydrate 323.9g, of which sugars 321.3g; Fat 169.1g, of which saturates 99.5g; Cholesterol 5mg; Calcium 1370mg; Fibre 0g; Sodium 2521mg.

Flaked almond bark Per total amount: Energy 2575kcal/10705kJ; Protein 60.6g; Carbohydrate 1475g, of which sugars 130.3g; Fat 197.7g, of which saturates 46.9g; Cholesterol 18mg; Calcium 611mg; Fibre 17.9g; Sodium 315mg.

Chocolate berry cups Per total amount: Energy 437kcal/1824kJ; Protein 4.3g; Carbohydrate 37.9g, of which sugars 35.3g; Fat 32.8g, of which saturates 18.6g; Cholesterol 48mg; Calcium 61mg; Fibre 2.5g; Sodium 21mg.

Chocolate coins with candied fruit Per portion: Energy 49kcal/204kJ; Protein 0.4g; Carbohydrate 6.6g, of which sugars 6.2g; Fat 2.5g, of which saturates 1.4g; Cholesterol 1mg; Calcium 6mg; Fibre 0.1g; Sodium 7mg.

Chocolate boats Per portion: Energy 126kcal/526kJ; Protein 1.2g; Carbohydrate 14.4g, of which sugars 7.5g; Fat 7.6g, of which saturates 4.6g; Cholesterol 19mg; Calcium 17mg; Fibre 0.2g; Sodium 41mg.

Mini chocolate brownies Per portion: Energy 228kcal/955kJ; Protein 2.7g; Carbohydrate 27.6g, of which sugars 22.6g; Fat 12.7g, of which saturates 7.5g; Cholesterol 49mg; Calcium 26mg; Fibre 0.2g; Sodium 62mg.

Chocolate tuiles Per portion: Energy 62kcal/260kJ; Protein 0.8g; Carbohydrate 7g, of which sugars 4.4g; Fat 3.6g, of which saturates 2.4g; Cholesterol 10mg; Calcium 9mg; Fibre 0.2g; Sodium 46mg.

Mini lamingtons Per portion: Energy 365kcal/1530kJ; Protein 4.1g; Carbohydrate 48.7g, of which sugars 40.9g; Fat 18.4g, of which saturates 13.9g; Cholesterol 48mg; Calcium 53mg; Fibre 2.9g; Sodium 46mg.

Index

Pubisher's acknowledgements:
The publishers would like to thank the following for permission to reproduce their images (t = top, b = bottom, l = left and r = right): 6b The Gallery Collection/Corbis, 7t British Library Board/The Bridgeman Art Library, 7br iStockphoto, 8tl Mary Evans Picture Library/Alamy, 8tr bilwissedition Ltd. & Co. KG/Alamy, 9tr Peter Titmuss/Alamy, 9b Photos 12/Alamy, 10 Museo de America, Madrid/The Bridgeman Art Library, 11bl Staatliche Kunstsammlungen Dresden/The Bridgeman Art Library, 11tr O'Shea Gallery, London/ The Bridgeman Art Library, 12t iStockphoto, 12bl The Bridgeman Art Library, 12 br Archives Charmet/The Bridgeman Art Library, 13tl Bettmann/Corbis, 13tr Yadid Levy/Alamy, 13br Leser/photocuisine/Corbis.

Author's acknowledgements:
This book was a grand undertaking that spanned more than a year. I have to thank, above everyone else, my mother Elisabeth Ptak. Not only did she cup her hand around mine as it held the spoon that mixed my first batch of brownies, she also taught me to hold a pen. She is my best editor and most ardent supporter. Thank you, Mom. To my father Gene and his mother, my grandma Bette, for loving to cook and bake, and always encouraging me on my path. To Louis because he is an awesome big brother and an inspired cook.

Thank you to Lucy Doncaster, my tireless editor, for believing in me the whole way through and always ending emails on a positive note. Your baby will be a born sweets-maker! Thanks to Nicki Dowey for her lovely photos and red bush tea. To Kate McCullough, my gossip girl xoxo. To Ana Freitas and Dri Nascimento for keeping my business going while I was writing this book and for being the best employees ever. To Tommi Miers for encouraging and inspiring me and for dancing. A special thank you to Fanny Singer for always helping me creatively and for gummy bear totems.

Lastly I want to thank Alice Waters for conjuring up a very different sort of restaurant in Chez Panisse some 39 years ago. Without my three years in pastry at Chez, my life would be vastly different.